CELEBRATING GATESHEAD

SANDRA BRACK, MARGARET HALL AND ANTHEA LANG

AMBERLEY

First published 2020

Amberley Publishing, The Hill, Stroud
Gloucestershire GL5 4EP

www.amberley-books.com

British Library Cataloguing in Publication Data.
A catalogue record for this book is available from the British Library.

ISBN 978 1 4456 9734 5 (print)
ISBN 978 1 4456 9735 2 (ebook)

Typesetting by Aura Technology and Software Services, India.
Printed in Great Britain.

Contents

Foreword by John Grundy

I really like lists; not so much lists that put things in order of importance but lists that contain snippets of information, the sort of information that has a chance of sticking inside my rather porous brain, the sort of information that I can drop into a conversation in the pub or at the dinner table.

I also like Gateshead. I worked in it (in Felling) for years and years and since then I have filmed in it and written about it, explored its rich and varied building history, driven around it, eaten its fish and chips, watched it change and modernise itself and been involved with many of its institutions … and so I like this book with its fascinating list of people and facts about Gateshead – I like it a great deal.

It has always seemed that Gateshead has had a tendency to get taken for granted. It has been that place on the other side of the river, or that place up north, or near Scotland but too rarely has it been properly looked at as a place in its own right and when it is, like it is in this book, you quickly realise that it's full of interesting stuff and interesting people, and the thing that grabbed me when I read it is what an amazing range of different skills, achievements and areas of life the people of Gateshead have been involved with. Some of them have been important in ways that you might expect to find in the North East: sporting excellence, for example, or the Industrial Revolution, making vital contributions in coal mining, manufacturing and the development of the railways. However, there has also been so many other areas of concern. There are artists here and patrons of the arts. There are successful women fighting back against the restrictions imposed by the male world. There are great entertainers, music hall stars, rock and roll artists and stars of television. There are several great scientists: you probably knew about Joseph Swan, the inventor of the electric light bulb, but what about Arthur Holmes? When I read Bill Bryson's *A Short History of Nearly Everything* I was delighted to find that it included that immensely important geologist from Durham University – but now I know he came from Gateshead, which is even better. There are philosophers, enlightened industrialists and philanthropists who pushed back against the darkness that blighted so many lives. So many interesting people, so many valuable lives!

It's a terrific list and it all came from Gateshead and it's just what the doctor ordered because we all need to feel proud of the place where we live.

Introduction

Gateshead, like all towns and cities, has much to celebrate. When we think of celebrations, national events come to mind such as the victory celebration (shown in the photograph below), the Queen's Jubilee or a royal wedding. We also think of local events that have been celebrated such as the Gateshead Garden Festival in 1990.

Peace celebrations Victoria Girls' School, 18 July 1919.

In this book of celebrations the authors look deeper into the town's past and present and focus on important events that have taken place, as well as other lesser-known subjects.

Using eight themes they have explored Gateshead's past, celebrating a wide variety of topics. They have looked at local art and artists, entertainers, song writers and musicians and a number of local heroes. They also celebrate some quirky facts, as well as taking a look at how the town has acknowledged its heritage through restoration and rejuvenation.

Gateshead Local History Society

Achievements

In this section we celebrate some acts of note. Some are by people who have achieved fame nationally but others are much less well known. Some achievements are major, others less so, but all in some way have made a difference.

William Moore Ede – Penny Dinners for the Poor

William Moore Ede was a prominent churchman who became Dean of Worcester in 1908 but was always remembered by members of his Gateshead congregation for the relief work he oversaw in Gateshead. He came to the town in 1881 as rector of St Mary's – Gateshead's main parish church. He soon realised the poverty in which many of his parishioners were living, particularly in times of unemployment, and he was also concerned that children attending local schools

William Moore Ede.

were literally falling asleep at their desks due to lack of nourishment. So, in 1884, Ede began an experiment at St Mary's National School where for 1*d* a day children of widows and the unemployed could have a meal of soup, pease pudding and either raisin or rhubarb pudding. When word got out, people came from all over England to see 'Moore Ede's penny dinners' – he even invented a special oven for cooking the meals. The system soon spread elsewhere. However, Moore Ede didn't stop there. He was soon advocating pensions for the elderly, producing 'A national pension scheme; or a way out of darkest England' twenty years before pensions began. His friend Robert Spence Watson later called him 'a great force for righteousness ... an example of the man who preached, but practised first'.

Brendan Foster – Gateshead's Gold Medallist

Brendan Foster, born in Hebburn, became Gateshead's most successful athlete after winning a gold medal in the 5,000 metres at the European Championships in 1974 and in the same year, a silver medal in the 5,000 metres at the Commonwealth Games, a bronze medal in the 10,000 metres at the Montréal Olympics in 1976,

Brendan Foster.

and then a gold medal in the 10,000 metres at the 1978 Commonwealth Games. Even a new public house, the Gold Medal, built in the 1970s, was named after his two gold medal wins and for a number of years one of his gold medals was on display there.

He will always be remembered locally for breaking the 3,000 metres world record at Gateshead International Stadium with a time of 7:35.2 in 1974. In the same year he became director of Gateshead Council's Recreation Department. In 1977 he helped organise the 'Gateshead Fun Run', then in 1981 he founded the Great North Run, which became an annual event of a half marathon from Newcastle to South Shields. The race is the biggest running event in the UK and one of the largest in the world, and celebrates its fortieth anniversary this year (2020).

In 1981 he became the UK managing director of Nike, then European managing director, Vice-President Marketing (Worldwide) and Vice-President of Nike Europe, then in 1988 he co-founded the company Nova International. He has also been a regular TV commentator.

For these achievements Foster was awarded the Honorary Freeman of Gateshead on 20 November 2004, given a CBE in the Queen's 2008 New Year's honours list and inducted into the England Athletics Hall of Fame in 2010. More honours followed. In 2016 he was given the Freedom of Newcastle upon Tyne and the following year received the International Association of Athletics Federation Golden Order of Merit – the highest award that the Athletics Federation can give.

George Hawks 'New Gateshead' – A Vision for His Workforce

George Hawks was the grandson of William Hawks, who had established ironworks on the South Shore, Gateshead, in 1748. George Crawshay acquired two thirds of the company in 1840 and the works later became Hawks, Crawshay & Sons. At this time the company was the largest ironworks on Tyneside and employed over 800 men. The company would go on to cast the 5,050 tons of iron for the High Level Bridge, which opened in 1849.

George Hawks adopted a paternalistic and caring attitude towards his employees, and planned a model village for some of his workforce in the 1830s. The cottages were designed by John and Benjamin Green, architects of considerable note, with larger cottages at the ends of the terraces for the foremen of the works. They were situated in Saltmeadows, near to the ironworks, and were known as 'Hawks Cottages'. A school for the workers' children was built later in 1832. Sadly, after only two streets were completed Hawks ran out of money. However, the cottages were so well built and architecturally attractive that there was widespread dismay when they were demolished in the 1960s.

Hawks Cottages, Saltmeadows.

Arthur Holmes – A Crater on Mars

From being a schoolboy at Gateshead Higher Grade School, Arthur Holmes, born in 1890, was interested in the age of the earth. When he was seventeen he enrolled at the Royal College of Science in London, now known as

Arthur Holmes.

Imperial College, to study physics, but, against the advice of his tutors, also took a course in geology. In 1913, he published his famous book *The Age of the Earth* in which he argued that radioactive methods should be used to estimate the Earth's age. At the time around forty million years was the estimate but over the next decades, as he continued to promote his theory, he earned the nickname 'father of modern geochronology' and by the 1940s he had revised the estimate to 4,500 million years.

From 1924 to 1943, Holmes was Reader in Geology at Durham University, then moved to Edinburgh University to hold the Chair in geology which he held until his retirement in 1956. Arthur made a great impact through his pioneer work on radiometric methods of rock dating and generally contributed to the understanding of the history of the earth and was able to write about his subject in a clear, easy to understand way. He never sought fame but influenced a great number of scientists by his writings.

To celebrate Holmes' achievements, both the Department of Earth Sciences Isotope Geology Laboratory and the students' Geology Society at Durham University are now named after him. Much further afield, he even has a crater on Mars named after him. Arthur Holmes died on 20 September 1965 in London.

Mawson and Swan – Photographic Pioneers

Mawson and Swan was a well-known and highly regarded shop in Newcastle upon Tyne but both original partners, John Mawson and Joseph Wilson Swan, lived in Gateshead.

John Mawson, a chemist, founded the firm at No. 13 Mosley Street, Newcastle upon Tyne, in 1839, which he described as a chemical and photographic establishment. Swan went to work for Mawson and both men specialised

Mawson and Swan's shop, Grey Street, Newcastle.

in photography, producing what was regarded as the best collodion (a chemical substance used to produce negatives) in the 1850s. In 1864, Mawson took Swan as his partner by which time Swan was his brother-in-law, Mawson's second wife Elizabeth being Swan's sister. The same year, Swan developed a carbon process known as the autotype, which produced permanent photographs. Mawson (who became Sheriff of Newcastle) died in a terrible accident on Newcastle's Town Moor in 1867, after which his widow Elizabeth became a partner in the firm and the firm became Mawson, Swan and Mawson, later becoming Mawson, Swan and Morgan.

Joseph Stephenson Ridley – Pedestrian Superstar

Joseph Stephenson Ridley was born on 29 July 1845 in Gateshead and was the seventh child of Matthew Ridley and Frances Stephenson. Although his brother George Ridley (see later article) is more locally famous today, Joseph was much better known during his lifetime due to his prowess as a runner.

Running as a sport was originally referred to as pedestrianism, referring to races that involved competitive walking but then developed to include running races, which began to attract large crowds. Ridley's first big win came in 1865 when he beat J. Corbett in a race of two laps at Fenham Park Grounds in Newcastle, winning £30. Over the next five years Ridley had varying degrees of success in

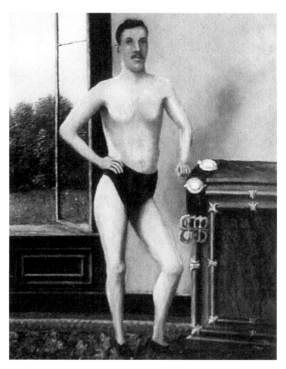

Painting of Joseph Stephenson Ridley.

short races such as the 880 yards but his real strength was in races of 1 mile or over. Large sums of money were awarded to the victors in the most important races, with prize money usually put up by wealthy businessmen or bookmakers. In 1870, he won a gold belt in a mile race at Manchester, but his greatest achievement took place the following year when, in front of a crowd of 12,000 at Gateshead Borough Gardens, he convincingly beat the famous J. Fleet from Manchester over a triangular track, winning the Championship of All England for the mile on 11 March 1871. For this he was awarded £100 and a silver belt. Running in a stiff wind, his time was a fast four minutes twenty seconds. It would be more than eighty years before anyone ran a mile in under four minutes.

Katherine Githa Sowerby – Feminist Playwright

In 1912, a new play was staged at the Court Theatre, London. It ran for four performances before being transferred to London's Little Theatre where it had a successful run before being transferred to the Vaudeville Theatre. The play was *Rutherford and Son*, and the playwright was the then unknown K. G. Sowerby. It was assumed that Sowerby was a man but when it was revealed that the author was in fact a woman, Katherine Githa Sowerby became an overnight sensation. But who was she?

In fact Githa, as she was always known, had ventured into print before, publishing a book of children's verse called *The Wise Book* with illustrations by her sister Millicent in 1906. She was born in Gateshead in 1876 and was the daughter of John George Sowerby, a notable local glass manufacturer. The play was a gritty, no-punches-pulled family saga, set against the backdrop of a glassworks and she wrote it on her family's move south when the fortunes of the world-famous Sowerby glassworks, on the banks of the Tyne, were in decline. Her grandfather was thought to be the inspiration for her brutal patriarch in *Rutherford and Son*, and it was through listening to her father's conversations at their Low Fell home that she learned about the harsh realities of business. It ran for a total of 133 performances in London before transferring to New York where it had a run of sixty-three performances.

The success of *Rutherford and Son* brought her financial security, which meant that she could support her sister Millicent, who provided the illustrations for Githa's books of poetry and short stories for children. She also wrote other plays but none achieved the success of her first.

On moving to London, Githa joined The Fabian Society and, while not a suffragette, she believed in equality for women. Although well known in the early twentieth century and regarded as a feminist, she and her works later lapsed into obscurity. However, the revival of *Rutherford and Son* in 1980 and other later productions has meant that she is now being restored to her rightful place as an important twentieth-century playwright. Indeed, the National Theatre regard the

Portrait of Katherine
Githa Sowerby by George
P. Jacomb-Hood, *c.* 1912.

play as one of the most influential of the twentieth century. There is a blue plaque commemorating Githa on a stone wall on Durham Road, Gateshead, close to her former home Ravenshill.

The Swinburnes – Town Clerks for Seventy-three Years

Gateshead's first town council was elected in 1835 with the offices of mayor and town clerk established on New Year's Day 1836. George Hawks was appointed mayor and had the casting vote when deciding on town clerk, appointing William Kell rather than the favourite Thomas Swinburne. Kell was succeeded by George Kenmir but on 1 October 1856 Joseph Willis Swinburne was appointed Gateshead's third town clerk, thus beginning the long reigning tenure of the Swinburnes, father and son that would last until his son's death in 1929. Before being appointed as town clerk, J. W. Swinburne had been one of Gateshead's town councillors and was a solicitor and partner in the firm of Willis and Swinburne, situated on the High Street, Gateshead. Joseph's son William, also a solicitor, was appointed deputy town clerk in 1891 and took over the office of town clerk on his father's death in 1891. William died in 1929 and the family tenure of office ended.

William Swinburne. (Courtesy of
George Frank & Sons)

Iris Alice Kathleen Waller – 'the most perfect example of English beauty'

When only twenty, Iris Waller then living in Wallace Gardens, Wrekenton,
Gateshead, was crowned Miss England in 1956, winning a trip to California
as part of her prize. Further success followed later in the year when she
won the title of Miss Great Britain at Morecambe, being judged by popular
entertainers of the time Dickie Valentine, Bebe Daniels and Sabrina. This time
she won £1,000. The following year she was favourite to win Miss Universe
but was placed fourth. When summing up the judging one of the adjudicators
said that she was 'the most perfect example of English beauty I have ever seen'.
As part of the competition she had to make a speech, which she did, all about
Gateshead. Success eluded her again when she was unplaced in the Miss World
contest. She later married an American marine and moved to California, where
she died in 1985 at the age of fifty. In the intervening years, she ran her own
interior design business and was a store model for the well-known American
store chain Macey's.

Iris Waller being received by the Mayor and Mayoress of Gateshead at the Town Hall in 1956.

William Wardill – A Climb to the Sky

Born near Pickering, North Yorkshire, in 1855, William married Annie Mandall in Gateshead in 1890 and the couple lived in High West Street, Gateshead, where he owned a musical instrument shop. He was first elected to Gateshead Council as a Liberal in 1895, becoming an alderman in 1909. Wardill became mayor of the town for the first time in 1914 and his second term as mayor followed in 1915. From 1926 he was mayor for three consecutive years, although during his tenure in 1927 he changed his allegiance to the Conservative party. During those three terms of office, he saw Tyneside's most recognisable bridge constructed. The new Tyne Bridge was built with two separate spans rising from the Gateshead and Newcastle quaysides. On the day the two spans of the bridge met and were joined up, Wardill climbed up a ladder to the top of the arch along with other civic dignitaries. He was seventy-two! On 28 October 1928, he was present at the opening of the bridge and attended a reception at the Shipley Art Gallery, Gateshead, with King George V and Queen Mary.

In 1929 he was made an Honorary Freeman of Gateshead and in the 1938 New Year's Honours was awarded a CBE for services to Gateshead, especially for his work with children. He died in October that year, aged eighty-three, and is buried in Saltwell Cemetery, Gateshead.

Alderman William Wardill
in mayoral robes.

Robert Spence Watson – Friend to the Poor

We celebrate Robert as a notable Quaker Liberal politician. He was the political agent for Joseph Cowen, MP for Newcastle upon Tyne and a solicitor in the city.

Born in Gateshead in 1837, he became secretary to the Literary and Philosophical Society of Newcastle upon Tyne in 1862, holding that position for thirty-one years. His work led to the society accumulating the largest independent library outside London.

The following year he married Elizabeth Richardson at the Friends' Meeting House, Pilgrim Street, Newcastle, and they had six children. Robert was one of the original convenors of the National Liberal Federation in 1877, and was its president from 1890 until 1902. He helped to found the Durham College of Science in 1871, later to become Armstrong College and part of Newcastle University, becoming its first president in 1910. He was instrumental in the founding of the Newcastle Free Public Library and from 1890 until 1911, Spence Watson was the president of the Society of Friends of Russian Freedom.

The family home, Bensham Grove, Gateshead, was visited by many important people – writers, politicians, entertainers and socialists – he was a great philanthropist to the people of Gateshead. He established what became known as the shoeblack brigade in Gateshead, which set up boys with equipment to clean shoes and thus gain a living.

At his death a newspaper report said that 'Never was there a man in whom the passion for human right and justice burned with greater fervour. He was an advocate of peace among nations, of justice at home, of the real elevation of the poor and oppressed, and he saw in politics the means to his goal in all these things'.

Portrait of Robert Spence Watson.

2

Some Gateshead Firsts

Gateshead has led the field in some surprising ways – here are just a few of them.

Bensham Grove Nursery – First Nursery in the North East of England

Bensham Grove was the home of Robert and Elizabeth Spence Watson, Quakers and philanthropists. After Elizabeth's death in 1919 the house was left to the community to provide 'a centre for education, social and recreational activities'. It became an educational settlement and in an early report it was noted that some women were running a nursery for young children. It was not until 1929, however, that the idea was put on a more formal footing with the foundation of the Tyneside Nursery School Association. The association decided that Bensham Grove would be a suitable site for the new nursery, which was originally based in the hall attached to the house. It was opened by Lady Trevelyan in 1929. The hall was not really suitable for a nursery and so, with the help of grants from the Board of Education and £1,200 from Lady Astor and her son, the Hon. William Astor,

Bensham Grove Nursery, 1931.

a new building was built in the grounds of Bensham Grove in November 1931. Many children in the area suffered from rickets and malnutrition, and great emphasis was placed on the provision of a balanced diet. Both George, Duke of Kent and his brother, the Prince of Wales (later Edward VIII), visited the nursery. On the occasion of the latter's visit in July 1933 it was noted that there were fifty children attending, with a waiting list of over 100. The nursery school was taken over by Gateshead Corporation in 1939 due to insufficient funding. Bensham Grove Nursery still remains a thriving council run nursery today and in November 2017 achieved an 'Outstanding' Ofsted result.

Electric Light Bulb – Light at the Flick of a Switch

Sir Joseph Wilson Swan was born on 31 October 1828 in Sunderland and moved to Gateshead in the 1840s when he was apprenticed to John Mawson (later his brother-in-law), who had a chemist's shop and chemical works in Newcastle. During the 1850s and 1860s Swan, by now a qualified chemist and inventor, worked on a light bulb using carbonised paper filaments, but due to the lack of a good vacuum and an adequate electric source his experiments resulted in an inefficient light bulb with a short lifetime. Undeterred, he continued his research and in December 1878 he publicly demonstrated a working lamp in the lecture theatre of the Literary and Philosophical Society in Newcastle upon Tyne. His home, Underhill, on Kells Lane, Low Fell, Gateshead, was the first house in the world to have working light bulbs installed. The second house to be lit by the new incandescent lamp was Cragside, near Rothbury, Northumberland, the home of his friend Sir William Armstrong. This was the first to use hydroelectric power as a source of energy.

In 1881, Mosley Street in Newcastle became the first street in the world to be lit using incandescent electric light. Swan founded the Swan Electric Light Company

Joseph Swan in his laboratory, 1910.

Underhill, Swan's
home in Low Fell.

and started commercial production; he received the highest decoration in France, the Legion d'honneur, when he visited an international exhibition in Paris.

Swan's incandescent electric lamp was developed at the same time Thomas Edison was working on his incandescent lamp and in 1883 the two competing companies merged to form the Edison & Swan United Electric Light Company, known as 'Ediswan'. Swan was knighted in 1904, awarded the Royal Society's Hughes Medal, and made an honorary member of the Pharmaceutical Society. In the late 1920s 'Ediswan' became part of British Thomson-Houston and Associated Electrical Industries (AEI). In 2005 Gateshead Council unveiled a blue plaque on Underhill to commemorate Swan's achievements.

Gateshead Millennium Bridge – In the Blink of an Eye

When Gateshead Millennium Bridge was lowered into place by Europe's largest floating crane, the Asian Hercules II, on Monday 20 November 2000 it became the world's first tilting bridge and on 28 June 2001 36,000 people lined the banks of the River Tyne to watch it tilt for the first time.

The bridge was designed by Wilkinson Eyre Architects and Gifford and Partners at a cost of £22 million, and its concrete foundations stretch down 30 metres, anchoring it to the riverbed. Weighing more than 800 tons it can withstand a collision from a 4,000-ton ship travelling at 4 knots. The very top of the arch stands 50 metres above the River Tyne when in its normal position and when open the deck rises 25 metres above the Tyne.

Gateshead Millennium Bridge in its tilted position.

Powered by eight electric motors each opening and closing takes four and a half minutes. It's a clever bridge – it even cleans up its own litter via special traps at either end of the bridge each time it opens.

Mary Gunn – From Poverty to Power

Born in Sunderland in 1883 to poor Irish parents, Mary's first job was as a servant to an Irish builder. She married an insurance agent in Gateshead in 1904 and had seven children, only three of whom survived.

Mary Gunn pictured in mayoral robes in 1942.
(Courtesy of Bainbridge Art Studio)

She was elected to Gateshead Council in 1921 and also served, with her husband, on the Board of Guardians (the local organisation responsible for poor relief). She was elected an alderman in 1937 and in 1942 she became Gateshead's first female mayor. The following year she formally opened Gateshead's Little Theatre (see later article). As well as being Gateshead's first lady mayor, she was also the first woman to chair Gateshead's Labour Party and was chair of the Education Committee for many years. Mary died in 1959.

High Level Bridge – First Rail and Road Bridge

The idea of a bridge over the River Tyne at a higher level was first proposed in 1771 after the Great Flood had swept away the medieval Tyne Bridge. However, it was not until 1834 that the idea was put forward to build a bridge between Gateshead and Newcastle at a high level, which would provide traffic with an alternative to using the steep slopes of Bottle Bank in Gateshead and Dean Street in Newcastle. It would also be possible for a higher level bridge to hold rail tracks. At that time there was no existing way for a train to cross the River Tyne, and a rail bridge would allow a continuous East Coast route from London to Edinburgh. In 1842 the High Level Bridge Joint Stock Company was formed, which comprised engineers George Stephenson and his son Robert, who would design the bridge, George Hudson 'the Railway King', and the architects John and Benjamin Green.

High Level Bridge taken from the Castle Keep.

High Level Bridge taken from Newcastle Quayside.

High Level Bridge showing plaque to Hawks, Crawshay & Sons.

The scheme received royal assent on 31 July 1845, and in October of that year a house in Gateshead and a house in Newcastle were whitewashed as markers.

The idea of the 'double deck' with the rail on the top and road below, rather than side by side, was designed to save space and keep the bridge a reasonable width. Piles were driven deep into the river bed to make a strong foundation and the Gateshead works of Hawks Crawshay were given the task of supplying the 5,050 tons of cast iron needed. Queen Victoria, journeying south on the royal train, officially opened the High Level Bridge on 28 September 1849. The bridge was opened to road traffic the following year, and the cost of the whole project was £500,000. The railway on the higher level is carried by a beam bridge while the roadway is suspended from cast-iron arches. The length of the bridge is 400 metres and the roadway is 26 metres above high water. It was the first rail and road bridge to be built in the world.

Hoggett's Crisps – Putting Pickles in a Packet

Sunderland-born John William Hoggett established Hoggett's Food Products in 1924 in a factory situated near the junction of Redheugh Bridge Road and Bank Street in Gateshead. It was here that the firm made sauces, pickles and potato crisps. In the 1950s they introduced what has been claimed as the first flavoured crisps – salt and vinegar – starting a national trend. In 1958 a newspaper advert appeared featuring the crisps, described as 'a meal in a moment' alongside the popular entertainers Morecambe and Wise. The crisps cost 3*d* a packet.

Hoggett's factory.

Team Valley Trading Estate – From Floodplain to Factories

This estate, the first government sponsored trading estate in Europe, was formally opened on 22 February 1939 by King George VI accompanied by Queen Elizabeth.

Trading estates arose out of the depression. By the 1930s most of the major industries in Gateshead, such as the chemical works and the North Eastern Railway works at Greenesfield (Gateshead's largest employer in 1900), had closed. The whole of Tyneside had been designated a 'derelict' area and was investigated by the Ministry of Labour. The North Eastern Development Board was formed in 1935 and in October of that year they issued a report recommending the establishment of trading estates.

Two sites in Gateshead were considered, with the Saltmeadows area on the riverside in east Gateshead strongly favoured. However, almost at the last minute a decision was made to switch the estate to the Team Valley. The 700-acre site of the Team Valley was well situated for light industry, although much work had to be done to it. Traditionally pastureland, the site was boggy and subject to frequent flooding so was stabilised with millions of tons of colliery waste. The River Team, which meandered through the site, had to be culverted and cleansed.

Construction began in August 1936 with George Wimpey & Co. receiving the first contract to build roads and services in October 1936. The estate was built

Kingsway, Team Valley, 1938. (Courtesy of Philipson Studio)

Plan of Team Valley.

on a grid system with a 53-metre wide dual carriageway, Kingsway, through the centre, running north to south with a central roundabout. This was the widest road in England when built. Factories soon began to spring up – the boast at the time was that it only took seventy-five days to build a factory ready to move into.

Apart from factories, there were other buildings on the estate: two garages, two banks and a post office. Some of the firms occupying the first factories included Cadburys, Hunters the Bakers, Mellolite Ltd (lampshades) and Hugh Wood & Co., who made mining machinery. The first firm to move onto the estate were Havmor Ltd, who made meat pies and sausages.

Undersea Cables – Bringing Home the War News

The war was going badly in the Crimea in 1854 but it took time for news to reach British shores. That is until the laying of the 'Black Sea cable' between Varna and Sebastopol by the Gateshead wire-rope manufacturer Robert Stirling Newall (see telescope article), who had responded to an urgent order to supply and lay the cable. Receiving the order on 15 December 1854, within an hour Newall had negotiated with Palmer's shipbuilding company of Jarrow to commission a new iron-screw steamer, named the *Black Sea* in honour of its cargo. Working night

TELEGRAPH HUTS FOR THE CRIMEA. — Mr. Thomas Bowman, builder, Gateshead, has been commissioned by R. S, Newall, Esq., of the Teams Wire Rope Works, Gateshead, to construct for the Crimea, with all possible despatch, two portable telegraph huts, measuring 8¼ feet in height, 18 feet in length, and 13 feet in breadth. In about a week these wooden huts will be completed, and ere long they will be on their way to the seat of war. — *Gateshead Observer.*

Above: Newspaper report concerning the telegraph huts.

Left: The construction of the undersea cable.

and day, the ship was ready and loaded with 400 miles of cable by mid-January. However, the ship had to be put into port at Harwich 'disabled' and the cable transferred to another ship – the *Argus*. By April 1855 the cable was laid and it was not long before successful messages were received at home. The cable had been constructed quickly and relatively cheaply as only the shore ends were protected inside the cable sheath, with just the gutta percha insulation protecting the rest of the wire. Nevertheless the cable lasted for nearly a year and during that year enabled many more immediate reports of the war to be sent to Britain.

Newall had been developing undersea telegraph cables since 1850 and in 1851 his company secured the contract for the Dover-Calais undersea cable, following which they had so many orders that by 1854 sub-contractors had to be employed. His firm laid cables throughout the world and Newall's experience with colliery winding gear enabled him to design the machinery needed for the ships that laid his submarine cables.

Whinfield Locomotive – First in Gateshead and Second in the World

Gateshead has a long history with locomotive engineering and is a true 'railway town'. Richard Trevithick of Cornwall can be credited with inventing the first operational steam-powered locomotive, the *Pen-y-Darren*.

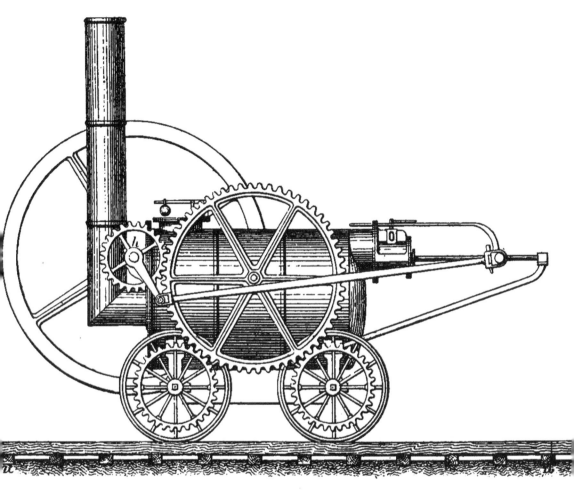

TREVITHICK'S GATESHEAD ENGINE.

Whinfield locomotive.

Christopher Blackett, the owner of Wylam Colliery, ordered a locomotive from Trevithick and it was built at Whinfield's foundry in Pipewellgate between October 1804 and May 1805. John Whinfield was an unofficial agent of Trevithick in the North East of England. The locomotive weighed 4.5 tons and could haul a load over 10 tons at 4 miles per hour. However, the weight meant it was inefficient and it only ran inside the foundry on wooden rails. It did, however, influence future locomotive design.

Art and Artists

Gateshead has a little-known history of art and art collecting yet it had two major collectors living within half a mile of each other, as well as a number of amateur artists living in the town. In the nineteenth century it had a school of art and in the twentieth century received its first art gallery.

Gateshead Stained Glass Company – Glass to Impress

This firm was founded by John George Sowerby and Thomas Ralph Spence in 1879 and was an offshoot of Sowerby's Ellison glassworks. Spence and another artist, A. H. Marsh, did much of the early design work in the style of

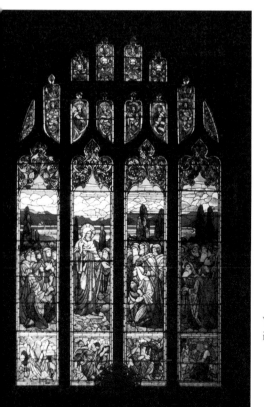

Window by the Gateshead Stained Glass Company in St Giles, Wrexham.

William Morris and the Aesthetic Movement. In 1882, the firm was incorporated with an art pottery. Its stained glass was fine but expensive due to the quality of materials used and by 1887 the firm was in financial difficulties. It was taken over by Henry Gordon Drummond, who had been a draughtsman at the firm but retained the original name. From 1900 onwards, the chief designer was James Eadie Reid, who adopted a more Arts and Crafts style for the designs. This was probably the period when the firm produced its best work. Sadly, however, the firm closed down in 1926.

James Leathart – A Pre-Raphaelite Patron

Born in Cumberland in 1820, he became managing director of Locke, Blackett and Co. in Newcastle, who were lead merchants. He married Maria Hedley, daughter of Thomas Hedley, a Newcastle soap manufacturer, in 1858 and in 1869 moved from Newcastle to live at Brackendene, Low Fell. By this time he had become interested in art and became secretary of the Newcastle School of Art. William Bell Scott, head of the school, encouraged him to buy works of the fashionable Pre-Raphaelites. Leathart began to commission his own paintings with both Arthur Hughes and Dante Gabriel Rossetti painting portraits of Maria. Soon his art collection had grown considerably and probably faced with the clamour of his fifteen children, he decided an extension was necessary at Brackendene so that he could have 'undisturbed contemplation of my pictures'. Thus a tower was added to the house.

However, while Locke, Blackett & Co. were the largest lead manufacturers on Tyneside, they began to experience financial difficulties due to foreign competition.

Portrait of James Leathart by Ford Maddox Brown.

Brackendene showing Leathart's extension to house his paintings.

Leathart was also having financial problems and was forced to sell some of his art collection in the 1890s, with further paintings having to be sold for death duties after he died in 1895. Today many galleries own paintings once collected by this Gateshead resident.

Elizabeth Cameron Mawson – Local Watercolourist

Elizabeth was born in Gateshead in 1849 and was one of the daughters of John Mawson (see the article on Mawson and Swan). She was educated at Bedford College, London, after which she took up painting as a hobby. She soon discovered she was rather good at this and painted a wide variety of subjects, although she is particularly noted for her flower paintings. She exhibited paintings at the Central Exchange Art Gallery and the Arts Association in Newcastle in 1878. From 1881 she gained wider recognition as her works were exhibited outside of the local area. She exhibited at the Royal Scottish Academy in 1883, the Royal Scottish Society of Painters in Watercolour and the Society of Women Artists in 1888–90, and in 1893 exhibited at the prestigious Royal Academy, London. She died at Ashfield House, Gateshead, in 1939. One of her paintings, *Holy Street Mill*, is housed in the Shipley Art Gallery, Gateshead, while Stockport Heritage Services hold another, *Tintern Abbey, Monmouthshire*.

Public Art – Art for All

In 1986 Gateshead Council launched its formal Public Art Programme attracting both national and international artists, resulting in an outstanding collection of over eighty contemporary art works. This has not only promoted the image of Gateshead but has also helped reclaim derelict areas.

Artworks can be found in the streets, at Metro stations and on the riverside, with each work being individually designed for its specific site and many having references to local history. *Sports Day* by Mike Winstone (1986) was the first of many in the programme and was originally coloured. Now painted black, the sculpture shows a punk in a sack with a hare and tortoise. Other artworks include *Cone* by Andy Goldsworthy, situated on an old foundry site west of the High Level Bridge, nearby *Goats* by Sally Matthews, *Opening Line* by Danny Lane at Gateshead Bus and Metro Interchange, *Acceleration* by John Creed opposite the Old Town Hall, and the famous *Angel of the North* by Antony Gormley, located on the site of a former pit.

Gateshead Council have received many awards for their public art programme including the Royal Town Planning Institute Jubilee Award 1990, The Arts Council/British Gas 'Working for Cities' Award 1991, the National Art Collections Fund Award 1995 and the Civic Trust Award for 2004.

Acceleration, John Creed.

Above: *Goats*, Sally Matthews.

Below: *Sports Day*, Mike Winstone.

Shipley Art Gallery – Newcastle's Loss Was Gateshead's Gain

Gateshead can thank local man Joseph Ainsley Davidson Shipley for its first art gallery. Shipley, who was renting William Wailes' former mansion Saltwell Towers, lived just half a mile away from James Leathart (see above). While both men were avid collectors of very different styles of paintings, Leathart's would be sold to other collectors and art galleries but many paintings that Shipley owned would remain in Gateshead. From humble beginnings in Gateshead, Shipley had risen to become a partner in a law firm and in his obituary was described as a 'self-made man'. He began collecting art from the age of sixteen and it is fair to say that he never stopped. He asked if Saltwell Towers could be extended to house his growing collection but this was refused and in consequence paintings lined the walls, floors and corridors of the Towers. When he died in 1909 he had amassed a collection of approximately 2,500 paintings – more than in the Louvre, Paris. As both his wives died childless, Shipley left a long and complicated will that included a bequest of £30,000 and his picture collection to Newcastle City Council on condition that they either used the money to build an art gallery to house the

Joseph Ainsley Davidson Shipley.

Shipley Art Gallery.

paintings or extend an existing gallery. The Laing Art Gallery in Newcastle, which had opened in 1906, was specifically excluded as Shipley regarded it as too dark. While Newcastle were deciding what to do, they called in experts to assess the collection. The resultant report was damning with many of the paintings being described as copies or 'of the school of' rather than the actual painter. A time limit of three years had been imposed on the bequest, and as Newcastle failed to make a decision, the bequest was offered to Gateshead, who accepted. They eventually selected the 359 paintings regarded as originals and added a further 145, making 504 in total.

The remainder were sold and in 1914 work began on Gateshead's new gallery, which would be named after Mr Shipley. The architect was Arthur Stockwell of Newcastle and the building opened during the First World War on 29 November 1917. The Shipley Art Gallery was listed Grade II in 1982.

William Wailes – A Window a Day

William Wailes was born in 1808 in Newcastle and is known locally for designing the spectacular Gothic Saltwell Towers in Gateshead (see Mr Wailes' mansion).

However, Wailes' national fame relates to the stained glass that his works produced. At the height of his fame his works were producing almost one new piece of stained glass every day, with Wailes employing some notable designers. His glass was installed in churches throughout the country and further afield – in Ireland and even Australia.

Wailes had started as a grocer in Mosley Street, Newcastle, but as the business became successful he decided to follow his first love, stained glass making. Wailes studied in Munich and visited many churches on the Continent studying the windows. One of his first windows was for Chichester Cathedral, but locally he collaborated with Augustus Welby Pugin on stained glass for St Mary's RC Cathedral in Newcastle and designed windows for St Mary's and St Cuthbert's churches in Gateshead. His great east window at St Mary's Church, Gateshead (no longer in situ), was designed to commemorate the fifty-three people who had died as a result of the Great Fire of Gateshead in 1854. In the centre was Christ with the four apostles on either side. These and other works have resulted in Wailes becoming one of the most noted stained glass manufacturers in Great Britain.

Portrait of William Wailes by Francis Oliphant.

Entertainment

The songs and music of our singers and song writers are well known worldwide and Gateshead has a number of local choirs, music and drama societies. In this section we celebrate a variety of entertainment.

Sydney Bacon – Success Starts Young

When the Metropole Theatre opened in Gateshead in 1896 the acting manager was the rather inexperienced nineteen-year-old Sydney Bacon, born in Bishop Auckland. Prior to his job at the Metropole he had been acting manager at the Queen's Theatre, Gateshead. Wheldon Watts, the owner of both theatres, predicted a bright future for Sydney. This was certainly true as he later went on to found a whole chain of cinemas in other parts of the country and was a member of the Executive Council of the Kinematograph Exhibitors Association. He died at his home in Muswell Hill in May 1927, at the age of fifty.

Sydney Bacon.

The Caprians – A Triumph from Gateshead Grammar School

This society was formed in 1953 by a group from the Grammar School who named their choir The Caprians, which was a derivation of the zodiac sign Capricorn – the goat, which was shown on Gateshead's coat of arms and was also the emblem of the Grammar School.

Members of the choir then formed an operatic society in 1964, calling themselves the Caprian Amateur Operatic and Dramatic Society. Their first production was *Salad Days*, which they staged at the Little Theatre, Gateshead, in 1965. The first pantomime presented by the society was *Aladdin* in 1967, again at the Little Theatre. Three pantomimes later it was realised that the venue was too small. In 1972 *Red Riding Hood* was produced at Heathfield Senior High School in Low Fell and since then all the pantomimes have been staged at the Dryden Centre in Low Fell, Gateshead. Like other local operatic societies the aim of the Caprians was to raise money for charities. The society changed its name in 2006 to the Caprian Theatre Company to reflect the shows they now produce.

Programme for the Caprian Society's production of *Belle*, 2016.

Felling Male Voice Choir – Trophy Winners

This choir was established in February 1920 with a concert in aid of Sunday School Funds for Holly Hill Wesleyan Methodist Church in Felling. From April of that year the name was the Orpheus Male Voice Choir. By October there was another name change – this time to Felling Male Voice Choir – which they have been known by ever since. They have competed in many music festivals around the country, the most popular one being the competition held in Blackpool in the autumn after the famous Blackpool Illuminations. The finest choirs in the country compete there and Felling were successful on many occasions.

The year 1951 was the highlight of their achievements when they won the Festival of Britain Trophy. This was held at the Festival Hall in London against fourteen other choirs. This trophy holds pride of place in the Mayor's Parlour at Gateshead Civic Centre. Other trophies won include BBC Choir of the Year, North of England Festival and also the Cork International Festival. They competed at the Llangollen Eisteddfod many times and in the Sainsbury's Choir of the Year were finalists at the Albert Hall, where the choir have also been guests at the many male voice concerts held there. The choir has also sung at many cathedrals around Britain and they have performed with some well-known singers including Sir Thomas Allen and Owen Brannigan and also with the Royal Northern Sinfonia Orchestra at the Sage Gateshead.

Felling Male Voice Choir, 1971. (Courtesy of the *Gateshead Post*)

Gateshead Amateur Operatic and Dramatic Society – Celebrating Songs on Stage

The society was established in 1905 with their first production – *The Mikado* – being performed at the Metropole Theatre on the High Street, Gateshead.

The president of the newly formed society was the Rt Hon. Baron Northbourne, one of the largest landowners in the town at that time. He held this title for some years until Lord Ravensworth took over as president until the 1930s.

The objects of the society, as stated in its first programme, were 'To conserve for the benefit of the Charities of Gateshead the musical and dramatic abilities of local Amateurs. They propose to perform each year a light opera of the Gilbert and Sullivan type. The whole of the proceeds will be handed over, less only the actual production expenses, reserving each year a small amount to carry on the work of succeeding seasons'.

The aims of the society in the present day, 150 years on, are much the same, with a donation to local charities from any profit that is made, although with rising costs for productions, the large profits of the past are just a distant memory.

In the early years of the Society the shows were performed in various theatres in the town. In more modern times with the demolition of these buildings, the shows are usually performed in the Dryden Centre.

The choice of shows has changed over the years – as has the name of the society, which is now called Gateshead Musical Theatre Company. Keeping to the original idea of performing Gilbert and Sullivan well into the 1950s, in the Society's Golden Jubilee Year of 1955, *Lilac Time* was staged with music by Franz Schubert. Over the next few years the society chose well-known operas, followed by operettas and finally the popular musicals that have been performed over the last fifty years.

In 1991 the society started a junior section for children aged eight to eighteen, which has proved very popular with local youngsters. Many members of the junior section have appeared on stage in the West End or other professional venues.

Crazy For You production by Gateshead Amateur Operatic and Dramatic Society, 2014.

KING'S THEATRE, GATESHEAD.

Proprietor—James Johnson.   General Manager—R. F. Douthwaite.   Acting Manager—M. S. Hammond

The GATESHEAD AMATEUR OPERATIC SOCIETY Presents

On MONDAY and WEDNESDAY, Feb. 17th & 19th, and SATURDAY (Matinee), Feb. 22nd, 1913,

'Merrie England'

Written by Basil Hood.   Composed by Edward German.
By permission of Messrs Chappell & Co., Ltd.

CAST.

The Earl of Essex	Mr. G. Macdonald
Sir Walter Raleigh	Mr. E. T. Heeman
Walter Wilkins (a player of Shakespeare's Company)	Mr. G. E. Patterson
Silas Simpkins (another player)	Mr. Fred Ferry
Long Tom ⎫ Foresters	Mr. David Ditchburn
Big Ben ⎬	Mr. Wilfred Walker
The Queen's Fool	Mr. Fred Patterson
A Butcher	Mr. R. R. Luther
A Baker	Mr. C. J. Robson
A Tinker	Mr. E. W. Robinson
A Tailor	Mr. E. Rosche
A Lord	Mr. W. McIntyre
A Soldier	Mr. J. A. McRoberts
First Royal Page	Master Norris Ferry
Second Royal Page	Master Roy McKew
Queen Elizabeth	Miss Marie Nicholson
Miss Bessie Throckmorton	Miss Eveleigh de Moleyns
Jill-All-Alone	Mrs. Colin Veitch
The May Queen	Miss E. Ferguson
Marjory	Miss Adeline Paulsen
Kate	Miss Bertha Young
Lady in Waiting	Miss Frances Moore

Act 1—Banks of the Thames. | Act 2—Windsor Forest.

On TUESDAY, THURSDAY, FRIDAY and SATURDAY, February 18th, 20th, 21st, 22nd, 1913, THE

'Yeomen of the Guard'

By Permission of Mrs. D'Oyly Carte.

Written by W. S. Gilbert.   Composed by Sir Arthur Sullivan.

CAST.

Sir Richard Cholmondeley (Lieutenant of the Tower)	Mr. W. Walker
Colonel Fairfax (under sentence of death)	Mr. J. Williams
Sergeant Meryll (of the Yeomen of the Guard)	Mr. D. Ditchburn
Leonard Meryll (his son)	Mr. J. Coyle
Jack Point (a strolling jester)	Mr. G. E. Patterson
Wilfred Shadbolt (head jailor and assistant tormentor)	Mr. F. Ferry
The Headsman	Mr. M. Ditchburn
First Yeoman	Mr. H. Alderson
Corporal of the Yeomen	Mr. G. M. Long
First Citizen	Mr. W. McIntyre
Second Citizen	Mr. J. Patterson
Elsie Maynard (a strolling singer)	Miss May Hopper
Phœbe Meryll (Sergeant Meryll's daughter)	Mrs. Colin Veitch
Dame Carruthers (housekeeper of the Tower)	Miss Marie Nicholson
Kate (her niece)	Miss Eveleigh de Moleyns

Acts 1 & 2—The Tower Green.   Period, 16th Century.

CHORUS.

Misses E. Armstrong, J. Adamson, M. Browell, M. Cleghorn, M. Elliott, H. Ferguson, M. Golightly, R. Hopper, L. Hildrop, C. Jackson, A. Moore, F. Moore, D. Magall, K. Myers, M. Myers, E. Parmley, M. Parmley, E. Purvis, S. Robson, M. Robson, C. Stobart, M. Stobart, H. Spark, G. Sykes, L. Shaw, F. Thompson, B. Tucker, J. White, G. Ward, B. Young. Mesdames Ridley, Tyrrell, Waugh.

Messrs. H. Alderson, E. Bell, F. Bell, A. W. Blake, N. Brown, J. Coyle, G. Cordes, J. Hutchinson, W. Hall, J. Haker, C. James, R. R. Luther, G. M. Long, J. McRoberts, W. McIntyre, V. Mills, J. Mackay, J. Patterson, C. Robson, E. W. Robinson, E. Rosche, J. Rennison, J. Reynolds, C. Ridley, J. Thompson, T. Todd, G. W. Tyrrell, H. Whitehouse, W. Heywood.

Conductor	Mr. H. G. Amers
Producer and Stage Manager	Mr. G. K. Veitch
Hon. Manager and Secretary	Mr. F. Favell
Hon. Treasurer	Mr. D. Ditchburn
Hon. Assistant Secretary and Registrar	Mr. G. W. Tyrrell

Silk programme for Gateshead Amateur Operatic and Dramatic Society, 1913.

Alex Glasgow – The Bard of Tyneside

Alex Glasgow was born in Gateshead on 14 October 1935, the son of a miner, and attended Gateshead Grammar School where he founded the Caprians choir (see article on Caprians). He graduated in languages at Leeds University and moved to Germany where he taught English. After his return to Newcastle, he joined the BBC and wrote the songs and music for the successful musical plays *Close the Coal House Door* and *On Your Way, Riley*. He is best known for his work on the hit television drama *When the Boat Comes In*, for which he wrote several episodes as well as recording the theme song 'Dance ti thy Daddy'. He wrote many songs, most of which were in Geordie dialect and some of which were political. Alex died in Australia in 2001. A blue plaque was unveiled for him in 2005, located on the house he lived in on Church Road, Low Fell, Gateshead.

Blue plaque for Alex Glasgow.

Brian Johnson – Rocking and Rolling

Brian Francis Johnson was born in Dunston, Gateshead, on 5 October 1947. In 1971 he co-founded the rock band Geordie, in Newcastle, but after a few hit singles, the band split up in 1978. After the death of AC/DC lead singer Bon Scott on 19 February 1980, Johnson was asked to audition for the band in London. Bon had previously heard Brian sing with Geordie and had told the other band members how impressed he was with his voice. The band decided that Johnson's performing style fitted AC/DC's music and asked him to join the band as lead singer. Taking over a well-loved lead singer's role was quite a challenge for Johnson, but the first album *Back in Black* reached number one in the UK and was regarded by some as the second all-time bestselling album worldwide.

In July 2014 Johnson was awarded an honorary degree of Doctor of Music by Northumbria University in Newcastle in recognition of his significant contribution to the music industry. In March 2016, Johnson stepped down from touring due to hearing problems. Then in August 2018, rumours began circulating that Johnson had rejoined AC/DC and on 28 January 2019, Brian Johnson confirmed that he was back with AC/DC and working on a new album. His autobiography *Rockers and Rollers* was published in 2000.

Low Fell Singers – Still Going Strong

The Low Fell Singers are a choir for ladies formed in 1941 as the Low Fell Ladies Choir by Mollie Peacock. Throughout their long history they have only had three

Low Fell Singers.

conductors. Mollie Peacock stayed with the choir as conductor for forty-five years until 1986 when Jean Stevenson took over as conductor until her retirement in 2017. The current musical director is Emily Murray, a native of Stanley in County Durham with a background of local music festivals, brass bands and county youth ensembles. She is also a piano tutor at Sage Gateshead.

The choir give concerts throughout the year for a variety of charities and organisations as well as singing at private functions and weddings.

George 'Geordie' Ridley – Celebrating a Local Songster

'The Blaydon Races', often nicknamed the Geordie anthem, is one of the most popular football anthems sung by football clubs who have absolutely no connection to Gateshead. However, the author of the words is not widely celebrated outside the North East.

George (later nicknamed 'Geordie') was born on 10 February 1835 to Matthew Ridley and his wife Frances Stephenson in Gateshead. When he was around eight years old he was sent to work as a trapper boy at Oakwellgate Colliery in the town, before moving on to the Goose Pit where he stayed for ten years. After that, he moved to the heavy engineering firm of Hawks, Crawshay & Co., working as a wagon rider.

It was while he was working there that his leg was crushed when a wagon went out of control. This meant that he was now unfit for heavy manual work and so turned to singing in order to earn a living. He specialised in writing topical songs in local dialect such as 'Johnny Luik-up' and the 'Bobby Cure' to existing tunes and, as he was a fine singer, became popular. He first sang 'The Blaydon Races' at a benefit concert for the rower Harry Clasper at the Wheatsheaf Music Hall – later called Balmbra's Music Hall – in Newcastle's Cloth Market. The song was about an eventful journey to a horse race at Blaydon, west of Gateshead.

He was a frequent performer there but then moved to the Tyne Concert Hall in Newcastle where he proved very popular. However, he never fully recovered from his old injuries and after five years his health began to fail. Following a short illness he died at his home in Grahamsley Street in Gateshead on 9 September 1864 when only twenty-nine and was buried in Gateshead East Cemetery.

A blue plaque to Geordie Ridley is situated on the wall of the William IV public house at the corner of Grahamsley Street and High Street in Gateshead. His brother, Joseph Stephenson Ridley, is also mentioned in this book.

Above: Grahamsley Street, birthplace of Geordie Ridley.

Right: Geordie Ridley.

Dixon Scott – Cinema Entrepreneur

Dixon Scott, the great uncle of Hollywood directors Sir Ridley Scott and the late Tony Scott, lived in Alverstone Avenue, Low Fell, Gateshead, with his wife and children during the early twentieth century and was a notable local film entrepreneur and cinematographer. In 1908 he established the first purpose-built cinema on Tyneside – the Kino at Jarrow. He went on to be responsible for other cinemas including the Haymarket Theatre in Newcastle and the Princes Theatre in North Shields. His biggest achievement, however, was to design and build a news theatre in Newcastle upon Tyne. This opened on 1 February 1937 as the Bijou News-Reel Cinema (today the Tyneside Cinema) at a time when there were already forty-seven cinemas operating in the city. However, this was the time of news-reel fever and the cinema was an immediate success. Today this is celebrated as the last surviving news theatre still operating as a cinema today, offering a varied programme of film, exhibitions and events.

Dixon Scott. (Courtesy of Tyneside Cinema)

Little and Large

From the smallest screw to the largest telescope, from a little theatre to the biggest shopping complex, we celebrate them all.

Dunston Staithes – Wood, Wood and Yet More Wood

At 1,709 feet (526 metres) long, the staithes are thought to be the largest wooden structure in Europe. They were designed by the North Eastern Railway's chief engineer, Charles A. Harrison, and cost £210,000 – a bargain considering their considerable economic success and built using North American pitch pine timber. There was no grand opening but at 6.30 a.m. on 16 October 1893, the steamer *Holmside* began taking on its cargo of coal destined for the Gas, Light and Coke Company of London. Within a year 1,259,000 tons of coal were being shipped from Dunston and due to this success the NER decided to build an inner staithe.

This involved moving the NER's Redheugh branch line slightly south to create a 9-acre basin capable of taking seagoing ships. This was dug out, islands removed, shallows deepened and a new quay wall constructed. The staithes were widened adding a further two rail tracks to serve the three berths facing the basin and opened in 1903. There were six loading berths (three facing the river, three facing the basin) with each berth being fitted with two gravity spouts. Three conveyor belts were later added. Loading could be carried out regardless of the state of the tide and all night working was possible, although until 1930 when electricity was finally installed, illumination was by candlelight. There were four railway tracks and with a gradient of 1:90 falling to the landward end, empty wagons could be run off into the coal yard by gravity.

Steam engines shunted the coal wagons on to the staithes 'blind', which led to at least one incident when a wagon became derailed at the end of the staithe and had to be rescued. The use of the staithes meant that large quantities of coal from the Durham collieries could be loaded directly onto the colliers, which transported their load to London or overseas.

The coal wagons were lined up over hoppers on the staithes floor and it was the job of the teemers to open the trapdoors on the undersides of the coal wagons and direct the coal into these hoppers. This could be difficult as the coal could jam, or freeze in winter, in which case men would have to jump in to try to free it. When the coal was frozen it meant that fires often had to be lit underneath – always a risky occupation, especially on a wooden structure. The teemers also had to link the hoppers to spouts and adjust the spouts by using a windlass depending on the height of the ships they were loading, although conveyors later helped. Once coal was loaded into the ships, other men known as trimmers (who worked in the ships' holds) had to level out the coal for stability. As well as coal, there were also occasional loads of fluorspar and pitch.

At its peak in the 1930s around 5.5 million tons of coal were loaded from here. After that a gradual decline followed and the staithes were closed in 1980, by which time they were the last working staithes in England. Extensive restoration work was carried out which enabled the staithes to be a major part of the National Garden Festival in 1990. Since then, however, a series of arson attacks have done much damage and the staithes are now on the Historic England 'At Risk' register. The present owners are the Tyne & Wear Building Preservation Trust, who continue to restore them. The staithes are on Historic England's list of the ten most important industrial heritage sites in England. They are also a Grade II listed structure and a Scheduled Ancient Monument.

Dunston Staithes, 1976.

Dunston Staithes, 1978.

Friars Goose Pumping Station – A River Tyne Pit Essential

Mining was an important industry in Gateshead but many pits didn't last long due to frequent flooding. The problem was partially solved with the invention of the Newcomen pumping engine.

The original pumping station at Friar's Goose was built around 1746 with two engines connected with Byker north of the river. Unfortunately the water proved too much for the two pumps to cope with and in 1763 the engines ceased work as they were drowned out.

A new Friars Goose Pumping Engine was erected in the early 1820s for the purpose of drawing off the water in the High Main seam of Tyne Main colliery. There were three sets of pumps, each 16.5 inches in diameter. Each pump stroke lifted around 195 gallons of water, removing just under 1.5 million gallons of water per day. It is difficult to imagine how this pumping station would have looked and worked in its heyday as now only a shell remains, which is Grade II listed.

PUMPING ENGINE, FRIAR'S GOOSE, NEWCASTLE.

Above left: Friars Goose Pumping Engine engraving by Thomas Hair, 1844.

Above right: Friars Goose Pumping Engine, 2018.

Intu Metrocentre – Originally the Largest in the European Union

In the early 1970s, Sir John Hall's company, Cameron Hall Developments, bought a waste site near Dunston in west Gateshead for just £100,000. Within a few years, the Metrocentre shopping and leisure centre had been constructed, financed by the Church Commissioners of England. The first phase opened on 28 April 1986 and once completed became the largest shopping centre in the EU. While this is no longer the case, it is still the second largest shopping centre in the UK, with 370 shops and over fifty restaurants and cafés that occupy around 200,000 metres² (2.2 million square feet) of retail floor space. In 1995 the centre was sold to Capital Shopping Centres (now Intu Properties) for £364 million, with the Church Commissioners retaining a 10 per cent stake.

There are five shopping malls – Red, Green, Blue, Yellow and Platinum – and three themed shopping areas – the Village, the Forum and the Qube. The Odeon IMAX cinema offers a choice of luxury, premier and standard seats across twelve screens as well as a VIP area, 3D screen and the first IMAX screen in the region.

Intu Metrocentre.

The Metrocentre also has over 10,000 free car park spaces, a Public Transport Interchange, and the Metrocentre railway station, which is part of the Tyne Valley Line running from Newcastle upon Tyne to Carlisle. Perhaps due to the involvement of the Church Commissioners, the Metrocentre is unusual in that it has its own full-time chaplain on site.

Little Theatre – Small but Perfectly Formed

The Little Theatre in Gateshead is aptly named as it was built on a spare piece of land that would have housed Nos 1 and 2 Saltwell View, with No. 3 being purchased and incorporated into the new building. It is probably the only theatre to be built in this country during the Second World War, which was entirely due to the generosity of sisters Ruth, Sylvia and Hope Dodds. It opened on 13 October 1943 with a performance of *A Midsummer Night's Dream*, which had music played by the Bensham Settlement Orchestra.

Over the years to ease overcrowding the theatre has been extended by the purchase of No. 4 Saltwell View in 1989, which houses a rehearsal space, coffee bar

Little Theatre.

and art gallery on the ground floor, and wardrobe storage and workroom on the upper floor. Then in 2012/13 considerable reconstruction and renovation work to the frontage, foyer and bar of the theatre was carried out, thanks to a generous legacy from a former member. However, the theatre itself remains the same size and comfortably seats 187.

The North Eastern Instrument Company Ltd – Celebrating Marvels in Miniature

In 1916, Norman Hall created a business in Low Fell with his brother Arthur. They called it 'The North Eastern Instrument Co. Ltd' (TNEICo), always known as the 'Factory' to the family. It was based on land the family owned in Low Fell, below the level of the main road, looking onto the arch of Carters Well, with access from what is now Well Lane. It was here in a small single-storey building that they manufactured equipment used in wireless telegraphy, taking patents out for some of their equipment.

TNEICo was instrumental in broadcasting the Greenwich Time Signal, demonstrating wireless telegraphy in the Northern Goldsmiths, Newcastle, around 1923. Also at Norman's home in Low Fell, Dame Nellie Melba was heard singing from the Marconi station in Chelmsford some 250 miles away. The apparatus used for this was an ordinary wireless telephone-reception set with a loud speaking device.

Originally the company was mainly concerned with marine work and the manufacture of ships' compasses and telegraph apparatus. Among other things the factory produced tapper keys used on ships for sending messages in Morse code. They began constructing crystal sets but much of their income was derived from a franchise they had for importing crystal (Cymosite) from France and selling it in little boxes. At its peak the factory was employing eight to ten people.

However, the advent of bigger firms and larger radios meant TNEICo couldn't compete and the far-sighted Norman saw no future for 'the little man'. It is not known where the inspiration came from but TNEICo began making parts for church pipe organ builders. With Norman's inventive skill and his brother Arthur's practical involvement, the factory became foremost in its field not only in this country but in Europe also. For many years TNEICo parts were found

The small factory of The North Eastern Instrument Co. Ltd.

in almost every cathedral organ in Britain and in many on the Continent. In the years before the Second World War the brothers became well known in the trade, producing minute brass screws that were accurate to thousandths of an inch.

During the war, there was a change in direction for the war effort. More heavy lathes and other machinery was imported, and the factory was extended and the production of microscopic nuts, bolts, screws, etc., were made as components for delicate instruments such as those used in aircraft. With the fall of France, Switzerland (which had until then been manufacturing these screws) was cut off and the supply ceased. The only factory in Britain producing the required class of work in volume, which was a Swiss concern, was bombed out. TNEICo suddenly found itself the object of much attention from various departments in the Ministry of Supply needing screws for planes, tanks, ships and submarines.

Organ work resumed after the war but now there was competition from electronic organs and it became inevitable that small firms such as TNEICo would be squeezed out by big business. Norman died in 1953, and after his death Arthur kept TNEICo going as long as he could as he didn't want to disappoint lifelong customers, many of whom were his friends. The factory finally closed in 1966 when Arthur was seventy-six. By then it was one of only four pipe organ instrument manufacturers in Britain. A sad end to a remarkable little factory.

Robert Stirling Newall's Telescope – The Largest Lens

In the grounds of Ferndene House, near Saltwell Park, Gateshead, could be found a rather surprising item. It was so unusual that even a king came to see it!

The house belonged to the wire rope manufacturer Robert Stirling Newall (see earlier article), who had a factory in the Teams area of Gateshead. Newall was a keen amateur astronomer, and in 1862 he visited the Great Industrial Exhibition in London where he noticed two large circular blocks of glass. He purchased these for £500 each with a view to having a telescope made for his observatory. At the time these were the largest pieces of glass in the world – nearly twice the size of the previous largest. Newall was determined to have a 25-inch refracting telescope, which would be not just the largest telescope in the world but also an English made one. At the exhibition he met an exhibitor, Thomas Cooke of York, who, on hearing of Newall's plans, became very eager to produce a telescope for Newall and bid too low in order to secure the contract, considerably underestimating the time it would take to make the telescope. As a result it nearly cost him his business. Also, construction was not an easy task and the difficulties may have contributed to Cooke's death in 1868, with the telescope being completed by his sons.

Because of the size, special equipment was needed to handle the glass discs. The telescope was finally completed in 1871 and weighed 9 tons and was 35 feet long. It was indeed the largest refracting telescope in the world and remained so for many years. The observatory used to house the telescope was designed

R. S. NEWALL'S TELESCOPE.

Above left: R. S. Newall looking through the telescope at Ferndene.

Above right: R. S. Newall's observatory at Ferndene.

by R. S. Newall himself and covered by a sheet-iron cupola 40 feet in diameter. It featured prefabricated parts, allowing for ease of transportation. However, Gateshead wasn't situated in the best position for watching the stars and in a letter to a friend, Mr Newall wrote 'In fifteen years of watching the stars in Gateshead, I have only ever had one fine night'. Leopold, King of the Belgians, visited Ferndene especially to see the telescope. Newall later donated it to Cambridge University Observatory in 1889 shortly before his death. However, it was not installed there until 1892.

It remained at the university until the 1950s before being donated to the Greek National Observatory. It is still there today, having undergone complete restoration as recently as 2013.

The Terracotta Army – But Not Full Size

During ten weeks in 1996, a surprising art installation was housed in former railway sheds at Greenesfield, Gateshead. This was *Field for the British Isles* – 40,000 tiny terracotta figures – the work of Antony Gormley for which he had won the Turner Prize in 1994. Nicknamed 'the terracotta army', it proved hugely popular, with 25,000 people visiting the exhibition. Many came out of curiosity

Field for the British Isles, installed in Greenesfield engine sheds, 1996.

as by this time it was known that Gormley would be designing a huge angel sculpture near Low Eighton, Gateshead, and it was probably after this that local public opinion began to sway in Gormley's favour.

The Gateshead showing of the *Field for the British Isles* was the first time it had been installed in a building that was not a gallery. The collection was later bought by the Arts Council in 1995. Antony Gormley was knighted in 2014 in the New Year's Honours list for services to the arts.

Local Heroes

Gateshead has had quite a number of heroes through the years although many have fallen into obscurity. This chapter seeks to address the balance as we take a look at some people who have made their mark.

David Almond – Persistence Pays

David Almond is a Felling lad born in 1951 whose novels for children and young adults are widely acclaimed. He went to school in Felling and fell in love with books at his small local library. He studied English and American literature at the University of East Anglia after which he had a variety of jobs including

David Almond.

working as a primary school teacher but at the age of thirty gave it all up to concentrate on his writing. For years he struggled to get his work published and it was not until his children's novel *Skellig* was published in 1998 that he got his break. The book was later awarded the Carnegie Medal, Britain's most prestigious award for a children's book. It has since been published in forty languages and sold over a million copies, as well as becoming a stage play, a radio play, a film and even an opera. He has won a number of other literary awards throughout the world including the Hans Christian Andersen Award, which has been described as 'the world's most prestigious prize in children's literature'. David is currently Professor of Creative Writing at Bath Spa University.

William Henry Brockett – An Influential but Forgotten Hero

William Henry Brockett was one of the most influential political figures in Gateshead during Victorian times. He corresponded with politicians and other notables of the day, and as a philanthropist he agitated for reforms to the town. One of Gateshead's first town councillors, he was elected mayor in 1839. After his death he left behind a vast collection of letters, posters, bills and other memorabilia. However, arguably his greatest legacy was in co-founding one of the best regional newspapers of the nineteenth century – the *Gateshead Observer*.

William Henry Brockett was born in Gateshead on 23 February 1804, the fifth child of John Brockett, clerk to the Court of Requests in Newcastle, and his wife, Frances Brockett. By 1827 Brockett had established himself as a general commission merchant on Sandhill, Newcastle, with a private house on the High Street, Gateshead. In 1836, he married Margaret Wilson, daughter of Thomas Wilson, the Low Fell poet and Gateshead councillor, and they had twelve children.

He had a great interest in politics and in 1830 was one of 174 signatories who petitioned parliament for reforms to the representation of the people following the election of Earl Grey as prime minister. At that time, Gateshead had no MP. The 'Association of Gateshead and Vicinity for the support of the Ministerial Plan on parliamentary reform' (soon abbreviated to the 'Gateshead Reform Association') was formed in 1831 with Brockett and William Kell (later to become Gateshead's first town clerk) as joint secretaries. Brockett supported Cuthbert Rippon, a Whig/Liberal, in his fight to be the town's MP.

Eventually success was achieved and in the Reform Act of 1832, Gateshead was allowed to return one MP to Parliament. This was followed by the Municipal Corporations Act of 1835 and it came as no surprise that Brockett should canvass to be elected to the newly formed town council and following the first polling day, on Boxing Day 1835, Brockett became a member for the South Ward along with his prospective father-in-law Thomas Wilson. So eager was Brockett to ensure a

Brockett memorial, Gateshead East Cemetery.

Whig/Liberal majority on the new council that he organised ward meetings at which he promoted suitable candidates and provided voting papers with the names of the approved candidates already written in.

Along with John Collinson, rector of Gateshead, Brockett was responsible for the founding of the Gateshead Dispensary set up in 1832 as a direct result of the cholera epidemic, which broke out the previous year. He was also the prime mover in the fight against the borough holders' attempt to retain their hold on the town's common land on Windmill Hills. This was a victory that later led to the establishment of the town's first public park in 1861. Brockett died on 15 January 1867 after a long illness. He was buried in Gateshead East Cemetery where his grave today (by far the largest in the cemetery) serves as his most immediate memorial recognising some of his many achievements.

Harry Clasper – Born to Row

Harry Clasper was born on 5 July 1812 in Dunston, Gateshead. His family moved to Jarrow where at fifteen he worked at Jarrow Pit but left following an explosion in the pit and was then apprenticed to a ship's carpenter. Here he learnt about woodworking and the principles of boatbuilding. His family moved back to Dunston and Clasper worked as a coke burner and wherryman and later at Hawks, Crawshay & Sons Ironworks.

Clasper formed a rowing crew consisting of his brother William and two other men, together with another brother, Robert, as cox and they were known as the Derwenthaugh crew. He also began to build boats for himself. The first was the *Hawk* in 1840, followed by the *Young Hawk* a year later in which he won the Durham Regatta single sculls race in 1842. In July 1842 the Derwenthaugh crew were beaten by a crew from the River Thames; it was here that Clasper realised that the Derwenthaugh crew's boat was much heavier and therefore much slower. He then built a new boat called *The Five Brothers* and attached outriggers to the side of the boat. Oars were then fitted on the outer end of the outriggers, which made the boat much lighter.

At the Thames Regatta in 1844 the Derwenthaugh crew narrowly missed winning the £100 top prize. The following year Clasper took another four-oared boat, the *Lord Ravensworth*, to the Thames Regatta where the Derwenthaugh crew won the Champion Fours, gaining the title of Championship of the World. The crew also developed a technique of sliding on their seats, thus producing a more powerful stroke. Many more wins followed over the next fifteen years. Clasper later worked with Tyneside boat builder Matthew Taylor to reduce the surface area and drag.

At a period in history when rowing was as popular as football is today, Clasper was a true local hero and proved to be not only a professional rower but, by understanding how the boat operated on the water, became a great boat designer and builder. In his later years he continued to share his skill and knowledge as a rowing coach and coached Robert Chambers, who became Tyne, Thames, England and World Sculling champion. Clasper died on 12 July 1870 and is buried in St Mary's churchyard, Whickham, Gateshead.

Harry Clasper.

Harry Clasper monument in St Mary's churchyard, Whickham.

Ruth Dodds – A Force to be Reckoned With

Ruth, the daughter of Edwin and Emily Bryham Dodds, was born on 8 May 1890 in Gateshead. She had three sisters and a brother. Her father owned a printing firm in Newcastle and was also an amateur historian. The family lived at Home House in Low Fell and Ruth attended Gateshead High School for Girls until the age of fifteen when she was sent to board at Clapham High School in London.

As well as being an author, with her sisters she loved the theatre and they joined the Progressive Players, which had been formed by Gateshead Independent Labour Party Amateur Dramatic Club. They performed at the Westfield Hall in Bensham, Gateshead, which wasn't an ideal venue for productions because the hall was used for many other things and the scenery and props had to be removed each evening after performances. This prompted the sisters in later years to finance the buying of a site nearby in order to build the Little Theatre on Saltwell View (see Little Theatre article). Ruth wrote a number of plays, mostly about the things she was interested in – history and politics. She was secretary of the Gateshead branch of the National Union of Women's Suffrage Societies and became more politically

Ruth Dodds.

active during the First World War, when she also worked at Armstrong's munitions factory in Newcastle. For a time she worked in the family printing business on Newcastle Quayside, but after a disagreement in 1926 with her brother over the General Strike, she left.

Although Ruth had political ambitions and was a Gateshead councillor, she failed to get selected as a parliamentary candidate for Gateshead in both 1931 and 1936. By 1939 she had resigned from the Labour Party over its support for the Second World War in line with her Quaker views. She was given the honour of being the first woman Freeman of Gateshead in 1965. She died on 1 April 1976, the last of her sisters, at Home House at the age of eighty-five.

Lettice Jowitt – Ahead of Her Time

When Lettice Jowitt came to Gateshead in 1919 to take up the post of warden at the newly established Bensham Grove Settlement she was breaking new ground. As the first and only female warden at the centre, she arrived in a town described by the Settlement founders as 'a town which is lacking in beauty, badly off for facilities for recreation, and backward in its education and municipal life'. She herself, however, always described it with affection as 'dear dirty Gateshead'.

Daughter of a rector of Stevenage, Lettice was the only child of a large Anglican family to convert to Quakerism. Educated at Cambridge University, she trained at a settlement in Bristol before becoming warden at Gateshead. She oversaw the merging of groups at Bensham such as the Adult Schools Association, the Worker's

Education Association, and outreach work from Armstrong College, providing leisure and educational activities to the people of Gateshead.

Lettice, however, was soon to show a sterner side and this was evident when she observed in her first report that an educational settlement 'must seek to unsettle those who had narrow personal aims and were content with the injustices and inequalities of the social system'. These strong beliefs led to a working relationship with Dr Henry Mess in 1924. Invited to Tyneside to conduct a social survey of the area, ten years later he ended up creating the first Tyneside Council of Social Services with himself as a director. Lettice Jowitt was at the forefront of his advisors. She was awarded an MBE and also became a JP for Gateshead.

In 1918 the Maternity and Child Welfare Act provided funding to councils, allowing them to train health visitors and midwives. Lettice took advantage of this and set up the first mother and infant clinic in Gateshead at Bensham Grove. The year 1929 saw the Bensham Settlement joining with the new Tyneside Nursery School Association and forming the first nursery school in the North East.

At the beginning of the Second World War Lettice was running a school in the Lebanon, and in 1942 she was living in a mud hut investigating the living conditions of Polish refugees in Tanganyika and Uganda. In 1955, at the age of seventy-seven, this amazing lady was teaching night school in the dangerous townships under the Bantu Education Act and showing total disregard of racial barriers and her own safety. She died in 1962 at the age of eighty-eight. Truly a woman to celebrate.

Lettice Jowitt at Bensham Grove.

Mike Neville – A TV Stalwart

Mike Neville was known throughout the North East and Cumbria as 'Mr Television News', having spent over fifty years presenting local news bulletins on both the BBC and ITV. His happy smiling face and the ability to keep going in times of equipment failure made everyone warm to him and many viewers felt they knew him personally as he was the friendly face in their living rooms around 6 p.m.

Mike was born in Willington Quay in 1936 as James Armstrong Briggs. After he left school he had a few different jobs before he became a full-time actor at Newcastle Playhouse in 1957. This was when he became 'Mike Neville'. It was while he was working at the playhouse that local television station Tyne Tees began broadcasting in 1959, just a week after the BBC began transmitting daily local news bulletins. Mike made his television debut as an actor with Tyne Tees Television in a children's programme. He moved to television permanently in 1962, still with Tyne Tees, but was poached by the BBC in 1963 to take over from Frank Bough to present *Look North*, a position he filled for thirty-two years, making him the longest serving anchorman of any of the BBC regional news programmes. He was involved with many other programmes apart from local news and presented national television programmes from time to time but always preferred living in the North East where he became a local legend. For many years he lived in Gateshead.

Mike was appointed an MBE in 1991 for services to broadcasting. In 2005 he was granted an honorary degree by Northumbria University and the following year awarded the Freedom of the Borough of Gateshead.

Mike Neville.

John Oxberry – Antiquarian Extraordinary

John is definitely one of Gateshead's unknown heroes. Without him, much of Gateshead's history would remain undiscovered and it is thanks to his research and collections that we know so much about the town. John was born in Windy Nook in 1857. His father, like many of the men who lived in this rather isolated spot, was a quarryman. As a child John trudged from Windy Nook to Newcastle Grammar School and home again – a round trip of around 6 miles. He led quite an adventurous life in his early days as he left England when only twenty-one to try his luck gold digging in the gold fields of Otago in New Zealand. Being unsuccessful there, he tried again in Australia but was forced to admit defeat and returned to Gateshead. He and his wife lived in Grasmere Street and from 1885 to 1890 he was the school attendance officer under the Heworth School Board. After that he was relieving officer under the Gateshead Board of Guardians, then from 1917 until his retirement in 1930 he was superintendent registrar of Gateshead Registration district.

However, he was also an active member of the Newcastle upon Tyne Society of Antiquaries for thirty-three years and held offices of secretary, editor and vice president before finally being elected a Fellow of the Society. He was also a member of Gateshead Libraries Committee for many years and was present at the openings of the Central, Redheugh and Sunderland Road libraries. Throughout his life John collected items of local history interest, painstakingly constructing scrapbooks of his research that he later donated to the library. He also wrote a large number of articles about Gateshead and Tyneside.

In 1937, he was elected an Honorary Freeman of the Borough and presented with a silver casket in the Shipley Art Gallery. John Oxberry died in 1940, still writing and collecting to the end.

John Oxberry.

James Renforth – Rowing to Success

Before football took over at the end of the nineteenth century, rowing was the popular spectator sport on Tyneside. The area produced three great rowers: Harry Clasper, Robert Chambers, and best of them all James Renforth.

James was born in Newcastle in 1842 but a year later, his father, an anchorsmith, moved the family to the Rabbit Banks area on Gateshead's Quayside. James became a smith's striker at an early age – a job which meant that he began to develop his upper body muscles – something which would be perfect for the world-class sculler he later became.

Renforth became interested in rowing and soon became proficient, probably helped by the fact that he was involved with ferrying men and materials across the River Tyne during the demolition of the Georgian Tyne Bridge in 1866. He eventually became such a successful rower that it was increasingly hard for him to find opponents on the Tyne. In 1868, he entered the Thames regatta where he beat the London champion Harry Kelley in a race, receiving the large amount of £90.

In 1870, he formed a crew of five men including himself to take on a Canadian crew at Lake Lachine in Canada. The British team won and were invited back the following year. In the meantime, Renforth had fallen out with his original team members so had to form a new team. Included this time was his former

James Renforth.

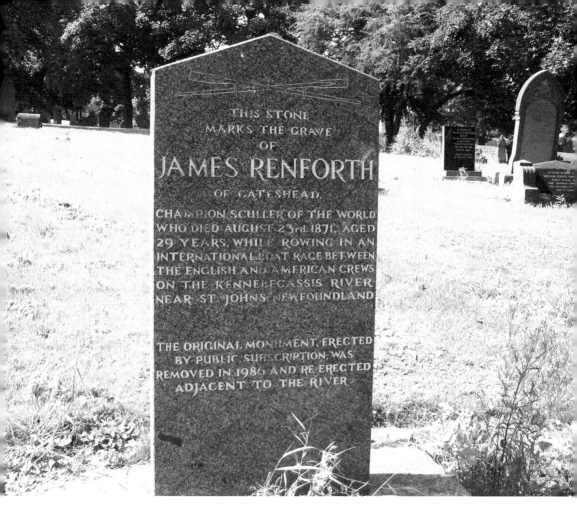

James Renforth's headstone, Gateshead East Cemetery.

opponent Harry Kelley. The race began at 7 a.m. on 23 August at Saint John, New Brunswick. The home team made a good start but Renforth's crew soon overtook them. As the Canadian crew began to fight back it was noticed that something was wrong with Renforth and he collapsed against Kelley saying 'Harry, Harry, I have had something'. The crew had no option but to return to shore where two doctors attended Renforth. Sadly, this was to no avail and at 8.45 a.m. Renforth was pronounced dead.

A post-mortem found that death was due to 'congestion of the lungs' but rumours persisted that he had been poisoned, although a more likely cause was heart failure following an epileptic fit from which Renforth was known to suffer.

His body was brought home to Tyneside for burial in Gateshead East Cemetery, in a triple coffin and packing case. A huge crowd of mourners attended his funeral – some estimates say 100,000 people. He was the third of the champion Tyne rowers to die in three years, following Chambers in 1868 and Clasper in 1870. His death at the age of twenty-nine seemed to start the decline in the popularity of sculling in England.

Andrew Wood – Gateshead's Religious Hero

Andrew Wood is a little known hero of his time. He was born in 1715 and studied at Balliol College Oxford. He became rector of St Mary's Church, Gateshead, in 1769 and was a popular incumbent. In 1771, there was a severe flood that would prove to be the downfall of most of the bridges crossing the Tyne. Heavy rain fell all day on Saturday 16 November and the level of the River Tyne continued to rise. In the early hours of Sunday 17 November the pressure of the floodwater hit the piers and arches of the medieval Tyne Bridge and by 10.00 a.m. the river was 8 feet above high water. The arches of the bridge could not hold the water and some collapsed along with the shops and houses that were perched above, with many people being thrown or falling into the river. Many onlookers took to their boats and rowed back and forth in search of survivors. Andrew Wood was one of the rescuers helping the victims who had been swept into the river.

Sadly the rector never really recovered from his exertions and he died of a fever on 15 March 1772. He was buried in the choir of St Mary's Church and after his death his parishioners paid for a marble memorial (now lost) to be erected in the church stating that he was interred here 'Amidst the tears of his parishioners'. Andrew Wood was regarded as one of the most learned and eloquent preachers of his time and collected a large and valuable library.

The great flood, November 1771.

Restoration and Rejuvenation

Over the years Gateshead has lost a lot of its history though demolition. This section celebrates areas and buildings that have been restored or rejuvenated for the twenty-first century, carefully and respectfully keeping a reminder of the past.

Baltic Flour Mill – From a Silo to Contemporary Arts Centre

Joseph Rank Limited opened the Baltic Flour Mill in 1950 at a cost of £1.5 million on the Gateshead Quayside. The building had been planned since the 1930s but plans were put on hold after the outbreak of war in 1939. The building had a short life as a flour mill – just over thirty years – closing in 1981. Most of the buildings were demolished but the original grain silo, which, when in use, had a capacity of 22,000 tons, was left standing.

In 1994 a young architect, Dominic Williams, working at Ellis Williams Architects, won an international design competition to convert the silo into an art centre, part of the money for which was from the Arts Council of England's National Lottery

Below left: Baltic Flour Mill during production.

Below right: Baltic Centre for Contemporary Art.

Fund who backed the project with £33.4 million for building costs and a further £7.5 million for running costs for five years.

There is very little left of the original silo building – only the north and south facing walls were retained, at a height of nearly 138 feet (42 metres). The east and west walls are now of glass, allowing panoramic views up and down the River Tyne. Renamed the BALTIC Centre for Contemporary Art, the building opened in 2002 with an inaugural exhibition B.OPEN. In 2011, the building was the venue for the Turner Prize. The art centre is unusual in that it holds no permanent collection. All art on display comprises temporary exhibitions. Also on site is the sophisticated rooftop restaurant SIX.

Central Bar – Celebration of Victorian Drinking

The Central Bar, located between Half Moon Lane and Hills Street, Gateshead, was designed in 1854 by local architect Matthew Thompson and opened in 1856 for Alderman Potts, a wine merchant, becoming a hotel around 1890. Its unusual five-sided shape has resulted in it being referred to locally as 'The Coffin'. The pub was used in the 1969 film *Women in Love*, staring Oliver Reed, Alan Bates and Glenda Jackson, and in 2017 the final episode of *George Gently*, starring Martin Shaw.

Unfortunately the Grade II listed pub had been deteriorating over a number of years, but with grants from Gateshead Council's Town Heritage Initiative and the Townscape Heritage Initiative funded by the Heritage Lottery Fund, it underwent a massive restoration project in 2010 costing over £1 million, following its purchase by the Head of Steam Brewery. This restored the building to its original Victorian splendour, with new chandeliers and stained glass and added a roof terrace. It is famed for its rather splendid Edwardian buffet bar with its original fittings, which has recently been transformed into a whisky bar.

In 2019 The Central Bar received the Gateshead Pub of the Year award for campaigning for real ale in Tyneside and Northumberland.

Central Bar prior to renovation.

Chemical Works – From Slag Heap to Sports Stadium

Gateshead International Stadium sits on the site of two large early nineteenth-century chemical works. Although initially successful, by the early part of the twentieth century both were in decline and were demolished in 1932. Their legacy was a 2-million-ton spoil heap. The land was later cleared and in 1955 work began to transform the site into Gateshead Youth Stadium. This was opened by the athlete Jim Peters in August that year at a cost of £30,000. Although only a cinder running track and asphalt cycling track, it hosted its first major competition, the Vaux Breweries International Athletics Meet, on 1 July 1961.

In April 1974, Gateshead's Sports and Recreation department was developed and Brendan Foster was appointed recreation manager. In this role he became the driving force behind the programme of improvements to the Youth Stadium. This led to the first Gateshead Games, which were a great success, becoming an annual event and giving the stadium credibility as a major sporting venue. The stadium was renamed Gateshead International Stadium and in 1989 its reputation was confirmed as a top-class athletics venue when it hosted the Europa Cup. The men's competition was won for the first time by a Great Britain team captained by Linford Christie and included Kriss Akabusi. On 30 July 1993, a stadium-record crowd of 14,797 watched Christie, who had won the 100 metres in the 1992 Olympic Games, in action again when he won in a time of 10.07 seconds.

Gateshead International Stadium also hosted the 2000 Europa Cup, which resulted in Gateshead being the first venue to host the event twice. On 16–17 July 2000, spectators at Gateshead saw Great Britain's men's team take the title for a second time.

In 2013 Gateshead was awarded the European Team Championships, and so became the only stadium to host the European Team Championships on three occasions. The championships were held on 22–23 June 2013 with Mo Farah winning the men's 5,000 metres.

Gateshead International Stadium.

The stadium can seat nearly 12,000 people and is a bowl-shaped arena with four stands of seats; the main stand is the Tyne and Wear Stand; others are the East Stand, and the South and North Terraces. Both the latter are open seating. In 2003, a new athletics track was laid in the main arena that has eight lanes in the sprint straight. The stadium does not, however, just hold athletics events. In the past it has been used to stage pop concerts and there are two artificial pitches for rugby, football and American football. There is also an indoor sports hall containing a playing area suitable for badminton, netball and tennis. The stadium is currently home to Gateshead Harriers and Gateshead Football Club.

Greenesfield – From Railway Sheds to Residences

In 1844 the Brandling Junction Railway Company, a predecessor of the North Eastern Railway, got permission to build a station at Greenesfield, overlooking the Tyne. In 1852 the adjacent site became the location for large locomotive sheds for the York & Newcastle Railway Company, and many of the famous steam engines that hauled passenger trains on the East Coast main line were either built or repaired there. Once the works finally closed after the Second World War some of the buildings were left derelict. Local housebuilders (Bellway) put forward plans to build apartments on the site and to convert some of the original buildings.

Ochre Yards is now a modern apartment complex, bearing no resemblance to its former derelict state, but also utilises some of the stone-built industrial buildings alongside the modern apartment blocks.

The names of the roads on the site were taken from some of the NER's chief engineers such as Edward Fletcher and Wilson Worsdell. The blocks of apartments were also given names of engineers, as well as some of the famous engines such as *Marmion*. A good example of a brownfield site coming back to life again.

Marmion – the locomotive.

Above: Marmion Court.

Below: Kenilworth House, Fletcher Road.

The Institute – From Reading Rooms to Restaurant

This is one of the smartest restoration projects in Low Fell, Gateshead. Built originally as a reading room, school room and lecture room by Thomas Wilson, a self-made local businessman, it opened in November 1841 with a grand dinner. Wilson raised the money by issuing five shilling shares, which produced about two thirds of the money needed, the rest being raised by public subscription. The building was then run by trustees but eventually began to fail and had a number of uses including being the home of a British Workman (a temperance bar) from 1879 to 1885. In 1923 Lloyds Bank bought the building, remaining there for the rest of the twentieth century before moving into smaller premises further along the road.

After standing empty for some time, the building was purchased by a local businessman and the basement, first and second floors were gutted completely. All internal walls were removed and the outer walls were taken back to the original stone. This revealed an old blocked-up doorway in the north wall on the second floor that would have led into the public house next door. The building, which is Grade II listed, was then sympathetically refurbished and reopened as a restaurant and bar.

Above left: Lloyds Bank after closure.

Above right: The interior during renovation.

St Edmund's Chapel – Prayer and Paintings

This building has one of the most confusing histories of any in Gateshead. We know that by the end of the twelfth century there was a chapel and hospital to the Holy Trinity in Gateshead and in 1247 the Bishop of Durham, Nicholas de Farnham, founded a hospital to St Edmund, bishop and confessor, which was amalgamated with Holy Trinity. The new chapel housed a master and three chaplains or priests.

In 1448 Bishop Neville gave the building to the nuns of St Bartholomew's Convent, Newcastle, as their nunnery had burnt down. In 1540 following the Dissolution of the Monasteries, St Edmund's and its land was surrendered to the Crown to be later bought by William Riddell, who built a mansion to the east of the chapel known as Gateshead House. In 1746 crowds gathered to see the Duke of Cumberland and his army marching to Scotland. Some of the watching crowd climbed onto the garden wall of Gateshead House to get a good view, but

GOATSHEAD MONASTERY DURHAM.
Published the 2nd of June 1789 by S. Hooper.

St Edmund's Chapel in an old engraving showing Gateshead House in the background.

St Edmund's
Church, 2019.

when the gardener tried to remove them a riot broke out in which Gateshead House was destroyed and the chapel severely damaged. By 1836 St Edmund's was a roofless ruin, and Cuthbert Ellison gave the ground and the building to the rector of Gateshead. A public collection was made for the repair of the chapel and the restoration work was overseen by John Dobson, the well-known Newcastle architect. It reopened in 1837 for worship as Holy Trinity with the only remnant of Gateshead House to survive, its gateway, relocated to the north-east of the building.

Between 1894 and 1896 the north wall of Holy Trinity was demolished and the building extended – the original building now became the south aisle of the new church. However, in 1969, the 'new' section of Holy Trinity Church was closed with the older original part remaining in use. Between 1979 and 1981 Holy Trinity Church was converted into a community centre, known as Trinity Community Centre, and the old chapel was renamed St Edmund's Church.

Today the building is still in ecclesiastical use on Gateshead High Street, with the old gateway of Gateshead House now situated outside the front of St Edmund's set into the south boundary wall. Since 2010 it has been used as a Sanctuary Art Space with a gallery along the north wall.

St Mary's Church – From Holiness to Heritage

Since December 2008, this has housed St Mary's Heritage Centre. This is a building that has a long and impressive history, surviving disasters, fires and cannon balls since it was built towards the end of the twelfth century.

At one time the church was surrounded by houses, industries and the railway. It was the only church in Gateshead until 1825 and although badly damaged during the Great Fire of 1854, was partially rebuilt. However, by the 1950s there was talk that the church, which by now had lost its resident population due to a vigorous slum clearance programme, should be closed. Refurbishments staved this off for another twenty years but eventually the building closed in 1979 after a further fire. It languished without a roof and a purpose until 1985 when basic repairs were undertaken by the North East Civic Trust. Phillips Auctioneers subsequently bought the building, opening it as an auction house in 1990, installing a new entrance directly into the chancel that they converted into a reception area. They also installed a mezzanine floor above the chancel and inserted galleries on the north and south sides of the church. Phillips moved to Newcastle in 2000 and leased the church to Gateshead Council, who reopened it as Gateshead Quays Visitor Centre where it showcased all the redevelopment work being carried out on Gateshead Quayside. With money from the Heritage Lottery Fund, Gateshead Council later managed to successfully purchase the building from Phillips and Prince Charles visited it in January 2004. From 2004 until 2007, the building was renamed Gateshead Visitor Centre and operated as a tourist information centre and craft sales outlet.

However, after further large grants it was decided that the building should have a new use and celebrate Gateshead's heritage focusing on the surrounding area. Features that had been installed by Phillips were removed and the building was

St Mary's Church following the fire in 1983.

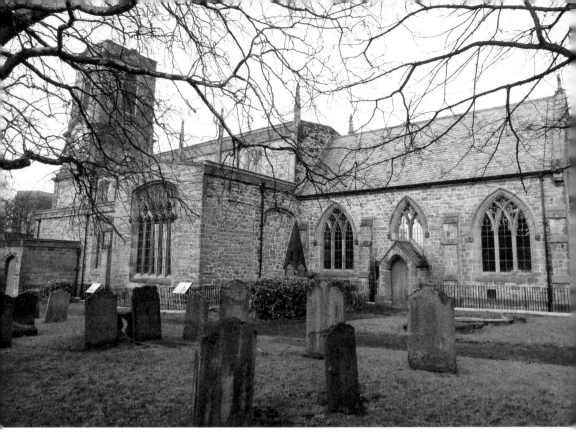

St Mary's Heritage Centre, December 2018.

stripped back to its basic shell, revealing 800 years of history. A heritage group to support the building was formed in 2012 and now the building hosts a variety of changing exhibitions, as well as conferences and other events.

Saltmeadows – From Chemicals to Commerce

The land along the river to the east of the town centre is known as Saltmeadows and was leased to Newcastle from 1555 for 450 years, by Bishop Tunstall of Durham despite opposition from the burghers of Gateshead, for rent of 44 shillings a year. The area of land leased increased gradually over the years from the original 34 acres to 95 acres by 1857. This became an important industrial area but didn't benefit Gateshead at all financially, although many Gateshead folk worked in the factories and coal mines here.

Tyneside's first coal staithe was on this stretch of the river and Allhusen's soap works was another large employer. Other large industries in the area were paintworks, ironworks, a timber yard, engineering works, chemical works, cement works and rope works. After these works closed the land that remained was heavily contaminated but over the last thirty years it has been restored to its natural greenery. The heavy industry has now declined and the Baltic Business Park is being developed on the site as part of the East Gateshead Regeneration Scheme.

Above: Allhusen's chemical works at Saltmeadows.

Below: Saltmeadows near to Friars Goose, December 2018.

Team Colliery - Mining Site to Metal Sculpture

Located on the southern outskirts of Gateshead in the parish of Lamesley, Ravensworth Ann Colliery, also known as Low Eighton Colliery and Team Colliery, opened in 1726. In 1939 a modern baths complex was built on the site, allowing the miners to wash and shower before leaving for home. After producing coal for almost 250 years Team Colliery closed in February 1973.

In 1989 reclamation work started on the site of the former pit head baths, and in 1990 Gateshead Council decided to use the site for a public art work as part of its Public Art Programme.

In 1992 the landscaping of the site was completed. The following year after asking for ideas from artists, a shortlist was drawn up by Gateshead Council's Visual Director of Arts in consultation with the Tate Gallery, Yorkshire Sculpture Park, Northern Arts and the Public Art Development Trust. In January 1994 Gateshead Council announced that the winner was sculptor Antony Gormley with his artwork *Angel*. The fabrication contract was put out to tender in February 1997 and was won by Hartlepool Fabrications Ltd, Teesside. By September 1997 Thomas Armstrong (Construction) Ltd had begun work on the foundations for the artwork.

The *Angel* arrived at the old pit head baths site in three sections in February 1998 and was slowly erected with crowds looking on in wonder. A time capsule was buried on the site in March 1998 and the *Angel of the North* was unveiled in June 1998. The *Angel* is a local landmark and stands 21 metres tall, has a wingspan of 54 metres and is built to withstand winds of over 100 mph.

Team Colliery.

TEAM COLLIERY. 1457

Erection of the *Angel*,
February 1998.

At a cost of around £800,000 the *Angel* caused a lot of controversy at first and today there are still people who do not like it. However, most local residents have fallen in love with it and it has now become synonymous with Gateshead and indeed the region. The *Angel of the North* is a fitting tribute to the former pit head baths site and the miners who worked there.

Mr Wailes' Mansion – Style Over Substance

William Wailes, a prolific stained-glass manufacturer, bought Saltwell Cottage estate in 1853 and later designed a spectacular house that was built between 1860 and 1871. The house resembled a cross between an Austrian schloss, a French chateau and an English castle in appearance using red, yellow and black bricks with towers, turrets and tall chimney stacks, surrounded by a stone belvedere, which, unusually, predates the house.

In 1876 Wailes sold Saltwell Mansion and its surrounding land to Gateshead Corporation, with the arrangement that he could continue to live in the house until his death. This was agreed at an annual rent of £140. The surrounding land became Saltwell Park in 1876 and was designed to provide a haven of peace and tranquillity for the working people of Gateshead. The house was referred to as Saltwell Park Mansion and later Saltwell Towers.

A later occupant was Joseph A. D. Shipley, a Newcastle solicitor who lived there from 1884 until his death in 1909. During the First World War Saltwell Towers was used as a hospital, after which it stood empty until used as an Industrial Museum from 1933. Unfortunately the museum was forced to close due to dry rot in 1968, after which it stood abandoned for years, constantly under the threat of demolition, becoming an empty, roofless shell, fenced off to the public. Then in the late 1990s a five-year restoration scheme started, costing more than £3 million, and in 2004 the Grade II listed building reopened to the public as Saltwell Park Visitor Centre and Café.

Saltwell Towers now has a new purpose hosting regular art exhibits and information about the history of the park. It also celebrates the history of glass art with an extravagant two-storey centrepiece screen designed by local glass artist Bridget Jones. Also located in the Towers is Bewick's tearooms, which offers a venue for events, meetings, functions, birthdays and wedding receptions.

Left: Postcard of Saltwell Mansion showing the belvedere walls.

Below: The outdoor café area at Saltwell Towers, 2019.

8

A Gateshead Miscellany

Our final section looks at lots of things in Gateshead that should be celebrated but do not fit neatly into any of our other categories. Here are just a few that we hope you will enjoy.

An Aeroplane in a Park – On the Ground Only

In Saltwell Park during 1982, an unusual feature in the shape of a former Vickers Viscount One aeroplane arrived. The aeroplane (G-AMOE) had first flown in 1953, having been built for British European Airways, and continued

Aeroplane in Saltwell Park.

for twenty years for a variety of airlines. On 15 July 1966, it was involved in a collision at Liverpool's Speke Airport. After hydraulic problems had been reported, the aeroplane was being ground tested but failed to stop, clipping the wing of another aircraft and continuing to travel, damaging two sets of passenger steps and a baggage trolley before driving into the terminal doors. Not surprisingly, the plane suffered extensive damage as a result. In 1972, it was owned by Northeast Airlines, who broke it up using the front fuselage as a cabin trainer for the company at Woolsington airport (today's Newcastle Airport). In its flying life it had flown for a total of 28,803 hours, making 24,429 landings.

In 1976, it was owned by British Airways and the front fuselage was married up with the tail section of another aircraft (Viscount G-AOHJ). The following year it was sold to Lambton Pleasure Park near Chester-le-Street and given a fictitious registration of G-WHIZ. After the pleasure park closed in 1980 it was transferred to Saltwell Park and renamed Saltwell Airways. In its first year it was visited by 22,299 people. It was removed in 1993 after giving pleasure to thousands of children who loved to play with the 'controls' and pretend they were really flying it. It was later sent to a scrapyard at Heworth and broken up for scrap.

'Amen Corner' – Holy Gateshead

Three churches once stood at the junction of High West Street, Gladstone Terrace and Durham Road, which meant the area was commonly referred to as 'Amen Corner'. The first church to be built here was Gateshead's second Presbyterian Church, the site for which was purchased in 1873 at the corner of Durham Road and Bewick Road. The church hall opened first, then in 1877 the church, which could seat 800, was built at a cost of £8,000. Although the church had very good attendance in the early days, gradually membership fell as district prayer meetings were set up in other areas. By the late 1930s the church fell into debt and closed. In 1940 the church was sold to Gateshead Corporation, who used the land for allotments, with the church being demolished in 1957, after which Gateshead's flagship hotel, the Five Bridges, was built on the site.

The second church to be built was Durham Road Baptist Church, which opened in 1877 on the corner of Durham Road and what later became Gladstone Terrace, at a cost of £8,000 and seating 850. Attached to it was a Baptist lecture hall and school building. Finally, to complete the triumvirate, the United Methodist Church was built at the junction of High West Street and Belle Vue Terrace. The site cost £600 and the church opened in 1883. Of the three churches the only building still standing today is Durham Road Baptist Church, which is currently being converted into apartments.

High Street West, Gateshead,

Postcard of Amen Corner.

Bandstand in Saltwell Park – Music Marooned

Saltwell Park has had three Victorian bandstands but the second one had a rather unusual history. Its original situation was near Saltwell Towers but was then moved to an area midway between the lake and the Broad Walk. People liked to walk around it and in doing so damaged the grass. The council decided to put an asphalt path around the bandstand to avoid this but people, being contrary creatures, ignored the path and continued to walk on the grass. The council decided action had to be taken and so took the unusual decision to move the bandstand to an island in the middle of the lake. This meant that the musicians and their instruments now had to be transported to the island. The move was not popular either with the musicians or the public and complaints were frequent.

One of the first complaints received was a letter from the Labour Representation Committee in 1910, who complained 'the performers were so far removed from the audience as to render many of the finest passages in the music inaudible'. When Felling Colliery Band were booked to play in the same year, they asked if they could bring their own bandstand with them and were reported as saying 'I think everybody seems tired of the band on the lake'. Complaints continued but the question of the position of the bandstand was finally resolved when an

Bandstand on the island.

extension to the park, the Grove, was opened in 1923 and the bandstand moved to its new position there.

Berlin & Frankfurt Streets – An Unpopular Choice of Names

Both these streets were in the Teams area of Gateshead – a rather monotonous series of Tyneside flats built towards the end of the nineteenth century for Gateshead working classes in a space-saving grid pattern. There does not seem to be any particular reason why these streets were named after German cities but following a wave of anti-Germanic feeling during the First World War, it was decided that their names should be changed. Accordingly, Berlin Street became Chamber [*sic*] Street and Frankfurt Street became Clasper Street, thus commemorating two of the best Victorian Tyneside rowers, Robert Chambers and Harry Clasper.

Berlin Street.

Cholera Obelisk – A Sad Memorial

Cholera made its first appearance in this country in Sunderland, arriving in Gateshead in December 1831. It lasted until November 1832, resulting in 234 deaths in the town. The first victim was a woman called Mary Hymers, who lived in the Hawk Entry, a very poor area off Bottle Bank, who was memorably described as 'a rag-gatherer of depraved habits'.

In July 1833 at his own expense the rector of Gateshead, John Collinson, erected an obelisk to the memory of 222 of those who died from the disease. The 14-foot-high obelisk made of sandstone was placed in the burial ground of St Edmund's Chapel, near Old Durham Road. The main inscription reads: 'Here lie buried two hundred and twenty two persons who died of cholera in Gateshead from Dec. 26 MDCCCXXXI [1831] to Nov. 5 MDCCCXXXII [1832]'. A further inscription says 'In the midst of life we are in death, Watch therefore for ye know not what hour your Lord doth come'. The carving was done by Samuel Softley, a noted stonemason and sexton of St Mary's Church, Gateshead.

Cholera memorial,
St Edmund's churchyard.

Gateshead Flyover - Not Quite as Intended

When the flyover in Gateshead was opened on 1 September 1971 it was meant to ease congestion in the town centre by taking traffic around the town toward Newcastle. The idea was great, although it wasn't long before a few issues arose. Firstly, it was meant to take traffic at a high level over the River Tyne to Newcastle, but this section was never completed and the flyover truncates south of the Tyne Bridge. Secondly, by constructing the flyover, traffic by-passed Gateshead's town centre, which meant lost trade for the shops, banks and cafés, from which Gateshead has never really recovered.

Today as you drive over the flyover you can still see the road ways that suddenly end, as if the road has fallen away. In recent years there have been discussions about demolishing the flyover and building a new tree-lined boulevard in its place.

Gateshead flyover to nowhere.

Horses – Tails in Town

You could visit most towns and never see, or expect to see, a horse. However, during the 1970s and 1980s in Gateshead, it was quite common to see horses tethered alongside roads, grassy open spaces, in the middle of housing estates, next to bridges, metro lines, the shopping precinct and even in St Mary's churchyard. In fact, anywhere there was a piece of grassed land. People accepted these four-legged friends with a mixture of curiosity and occasional exasperation.

Over the years Gateshead Council have worked hard with horse owners to try to resolve the issue, as each horse cost up to £2,000 to remove. As a result of the Control of Horses Bill 2015 Gateshead has been able to cut down the amount of time it takes to bring formal action and so the problem has now almost disappeared. Most horses are now to be found in their more natural homes of farmland and stables.

Horse with old retort house and Dunston in the background.

Horse with the old Redheugh Bridge in the background.

Maiden's Walk Coal Drops – Coals from Gateshead

When we look at these often unnoticed features near the Sage Gateshead, we are celebrating Gateshead's mining, rail and industrial heritage. The coal drops were added as a secondary feature to the Brandling Junction Railway's Oakwellgate station, and were built across open ground held by Cuthbert Ellison on lease from the Bishop of Durham. Their construction date is somewhere between 1838 and 1844 and they were built using local sandstone rubble. There are fourteen coal drops in total, varying in height from 10 metres at the north end to 6.5 metres at the south end. The first six are slightly different from the other eight as they have broader side walls and step in slightly towards the top. They also show evidence of better finished construction. Each drop contained a timber chute through which the coal was channelled using a simple gravity system. Some of the arches have a recessed section, where a man would stand to help the coal along its way, quite a dangerous job as tons of coal rushed down the chutes.

The coal drops did not, however, as has previously been thought, serve the incline to the quay. They were an independent facility to the station, presumably providing a land-sale outlet for coals and lime, without any physical connection to the incline, which began on the north side of Oakwellgate station. Today the coal drops are Grade II listed and remain a fantastic reminder of our industrial heritage.

Maiden's
Walk Coal
Drops.

Swing Bridge Pillar – A Stone Oddity

The Swing Bridge was built between 1868 and 1876 on the site of three former bridges joining Bottle Bank in Gateshead to Sandhill in Newcastle. There was a need for a bridge that was either at a higher level or that could open to allow the passage down river of larger vessels that could be built at Armstrong & Co. at Elswick further up river and to ease the transport of coal down to Newcastle Quayside. The Swing Bridge was designed and constructed by Sir W. G. Armstrong and was opened for road traffic on 25 June 1876 and river traffic in July. The bridge has four large pillars at each end of the footpaths. What is unusual is

Swing Bridge and Bridge Street, 1924.

Left: Swing Bridge half pillar in close-up.

Below: Swing Bridge pillar from the Quayside.

the size of one of them at the Gateshead end of the bridge. While the four at the Newcastle end are all the same size, the four at the Gateshead end are not; three are the same size but one is only half as wide. On closer inspection it is obvious that this pillar was originally built the same size as the other three. The reverse side shows a plaque with part of a castle inside a crest with scrolled edges and the last letters of the name Gateshead below. It seems likely that it was cut in half when a building (now demolished) was built onto it.

Trollope Mausoleum – Making a Statement

Robert Trollope, a seventeenth-century Yorkshire-born architect, worked mainly in Northumberland and Durham. His best-known local building is Newcastle's Guildhall on Sandhill, which he rebuilt in 1655. Trollope, who died in 1686,

Trollope Mausoleum,
St Mary's churchyard.

also designed his own mausoleum, which is situated in St Mary's churchyard, Gateshead. According to legend, near it was a statue of Trollope pointing towards the Guildhall accompanied by these lines of doggerel verse: 'Here lies Robert Trollope, Who made yon stones roll up, When death took his soul up, His body filled this hole up'.

The mausoleum was dismantled and rebuilt in 1850 in an identical style by Trollope's distant relatives, the Greene family, who were merchants and chandlers in Gateshead. The Trollope Mausoleum remains the largest and most imposing memorial in the graveyard today and is Grade II listed.

Tyne Bridge Public Conveniences – Lavish Loos

As you drive or walk over the Tyne Bridge into Gateshead notice the fine octagonal-shaped stone building on the left just before the entrance to Church Street. This elegant Grade II listed building is currently an architect's premises, but it was built in the late 1920s as a public convenience. It has two large oak-panelled doors with beautiful fanlights that lead to the ground-floor level. Above the front

Tyne Bridge public conveniences.

door is the old Gateshead coat of arms and the rear door is reached by steps off Church Street. The north and south walls each have an arched window and steps leading down to the conveniences on a lower level. The building is surrounded by wrought-iron handrails that continue down the staircases. Internally, the ground level was oak panelled and the lavatories were tiled.

Whitey the Cockatoo – Dead but Not Forgotten

Whitey was a much-loved inhabitant of Saltwell Park, Gateshead. He was also the longest lived – a remnant of the Victorian age – and when his end came and he fell off his perch, the council decided that he should remain as a stuffed specimen. However, they soon ran into trouble as the taxidermists at Newcastle's Hancock Museum were unable to carry out the work and it was decided to send it to a firm at Doncaster. Between its demise and eventual transportation to the taxidermists it was important the bird was kept in a state of preservation and not allowed to decay. The Queen Elizabeth Hospital in Gateshead refused to allow it to stay in their morgue so an urgent appeal went out to see if anyone had a spare fridge – an appeal that was eventually successful. After the bird was stuffed, it was donated to the Shipley Art Gallery where it was given pride of place in the curator's office. Today, however, the whereabouts of this aged bird are unknown.

Whitey the cockatoo in the Shipley Art Gallery.

Acknowledgements

We would like to thank everyone who has helped us in any way while writing this book. We are grateful to Eileen Barrass, Jen Bell, Shirley Brown, Trevor Ermel, Roger Fern, Christopher Newall, Brian Ridley, Tom Stafford, Maggie Thacker, Diane Ward and Helen Ward. Special thanks go to John Grundy for writing the foreword, Duncan Hall for his restoration of some of the images, and the Tyneside Cinema for their assistance with the image of Dixon Scott.

About the Authors

The authors have thoroughly enjoyed writing *Celebrating Gateshead*, which is their third book for Amberley Publishing. Their first book, *Gateshead From Old Photographs*, was published in 2015, and their second, *A–Z of Gateshead*, was published more recently in 2018.

Sandra Brack has been interested in local history for over thirty years and is secretary of Gateshead Local History Society. She is the author and co-author of two books on Gateshead's grand houses, and co-author of three walking history books of Gateshead.

Margaret Hall has lived in Gateshead for well over fifty years, and her family history in Gateshead goes back to the 1870s. Before retirement she worked for forty years for BBC Television on the local evening magazine programme 'Look North'.

Anthea Lang has published a number of local history books and writes text for the Alan Godfrey series of historic Ordnance Survey maps. She is also a local tour guide and an adult education tutor. She worked for Gateshead Libraries for twenty-five years, which is where her interest in local history began.